# IMPLEI
# TECHNOLOGY
# SOLUTIONS
## IN LIBRARIES

**Techniques, Tools, and Tips From The Trenches**

Karen C. Knox

**Information Today, Inc.**
**Medford, New Jersey**

*First Printing, 2011*

*Implementing Technology Solutions in Libraries: Techniques, Tools, and Tips From the Trenches*

Copyright © 2011 by Karen C. Knox

### Library of Congress Cataloging-in-Publication Data

Knox, Karen C., 1976-
    Implementing technology solutions in libraries : techniques, tools, and tips from the trenches / Karen C. Knox.
        pages cm.
    Includes bibliographical references and index.
        ISBN 978-1-57387-403-8
1.  Libraries--Information technology--Planning.  2.  Public libraries--Information technology--United States--Planning--Case studies.  I.  Title
    Z678.9.K585 2011
    025.00285--dc22

                                                                    2010047786

Printed and bound in the United States of America.

President and CEO: Thomas H. Hogan, Sr.
Editor-in-Chief and Publisher: John B. Bryans
Managing Editor: Amy M. Reeve
Project Editor: Rachel Singer Gordon
VP Graphics and Production: M. Heide Dengler
Book Designer: Kara Mia Jalkowski
Cover Designer: Danielle Nicotra

**www.infotoday.com**

*To my dad and my sister,*
*who left this world all too soon*
*but whose influence in my life will shine on forever*

# Contents

# Acknowledgments

As this is my first published book, I have a large number of people to thank, and I am sure my publisher would never allow me the space to print each name individually. But know that I could never have finished this without the support and encouragement of all of you.

First, I want to thank Rachel Singer Gordon, my editor. She got me into this gig, and she has been a trusted and respected colleague for a number of years. I will always be grateful for her support. In addition, I want to express my appreciation to John Bryans, Amy Reeve, and the staff of Information Today, Inc., for this opportunity.

Second, I want to thank all of my colleagues who have helped to shape my career to this point. I am grateful to have so many people in my network, and I hope you know who you are and how important you are to me. In particular, I must put in a special note of thanks to Anatoliy for assistance with my website and to Pauline, Brenda, Mary Ellen, Barb, Christine, Cathy, and Larry.

Third, I want to thank all of the vendors with whom I have had the pleasure of working over the years and, in particular, those at the companies I respect most, including Polaris Library Systems, EnvisionWare, Inc., Knight Technology Group, and Evanced Solutions.

And finally, I want to thank all of my family and friends for their support in this project and in everything else that I do: Mom, David, Annie, Mark G., Mitchell, Karl, Sue, Alana, Ellie, Katie, Kelly, Mark T., Sallie, and Michael. I love you all.

# About the Website
## www.karencknox.com/itsil

Information about *Implementing Technology Solutions in Libraries* can be found on the author's website, www.karencknox.com/itsil. All the resources referenced in the book are available there, as well as electronic copies of the documents in the appendices. Updated content related to this book will also be posted on the website. The author welcomes comments and questions at karen@karencknox.com.

## Disclaimer

Neither the publisher nor the author make any claim as to the results that may be obtained through the use of this webpage or of any of the internet resources it references or links to. Neither publisher nor author will be held liable for any results, or lack thereof, obtained by the use of this page or any of its links; for any third-party charges; or for any hardware, software, or other problems that may occur as the result of using it. This webpage is subject to change or discontinuation without notice at the discretion of the publisher and author.

# Today's Technology

We are inundated with advertising for the latest and greatest technology available to consumers every day. From cell phones to Wi-Fi to digital cameras and more, the technology revolution continues and challenges each of us to keep up with it. Social networking, podcasting, and texting are a regular part of daily life. Some consumers are out on the leading edge of technological change while others struggle to catch on to the tail end as it goes by. What does it all mean for each of us today? And what does the future hold?

Consumers are in a unique position in this technological revolution. Some are able to explore the new technology as it reveals itself to us. Many have to plan ahead and save money until they are able to afford a new device. And others are left trying to stay connected without the newest technologies, which is becoming harder and harder to do.

Perhaps one of the most widespread changes in technology was brought about by the Digital TV Transition in June 2009. This transition affected everyone who had a television and wanted to continue to have access to television programming. Analog television is no longer broadcast over the air. Every viewer needs one of the following: an analog converter box on each television set, a digital television set, and/or a subscription to a cable or satellite television provider of broadcasting.[1] This may have been one of the first occasions where everyone in the country was required to update to a newer technology in order to continue accessing something we previously had taken for granted.

With the rate of change in technology in the 21st century, these types of events will likely recur. Change occurs exponentially with internet technologies. Each year, more and more people use the internet for various services, and more and more services are available on the internet. The staff at the Pew Internet & American Life Project regularly reviews the use of the internet by Americans. In a 2009 report that analyzed Americans' use of the internet and its implications for libraries, it was reported that

79 percent of adults in America use the internet, 69 percent of online Americans have used cloud computing, and 56 percent have accessed the internet wirelessly.[2] Of those Americans who use the internet, more are reading and writing email, researching information, checking the weather, and buying products. Fewer Americans use newer technologies such as Twitter, blogs, podcasts, and peer-to-peer file sharing networks.[3] But these numbers change every year, as the users and the technologies evolve.

Libraries must serve consumers at both ends of the spectrum and everywhere in between. Some libraries are lucky enough to have funding to support experimenting with the latest technology. However, many libraries struggle with funding, and the problem has increased in the past few years as the national economy has suffered.

The American Library Association (ALA) recently published a report titled, "The Condition of U.S. Libraries: Trends, 1999–2009," written by Denise M. Davis, director of the ALA Office for Research and Statistics. This report includes statistics about public libraries, school libraries, and academic libraries, as well as those organizations that provide services to libraries (library networks, cooperatives, and consortia). First, Davis notes that "American households reported using their public libraries more often in 2009," and that more than 90 percent of Americans recognize the value of all types of libraries in their communities. However, she also notes the budgetary impact of the economic downturn beginning in 2008. "Flat funding has been an obstacle—perhaps even a chronic problem—for many libraries this entire decade."[4] Certainly, it is no secret that the situation is worsening with budget cuts at every level, affecting public, school, and academic libraries.

Libraries must make tough decisions about where to spend their limited funds. Very few libraries can afford to purchase and implement all the latest technology whenever it becomes available. In reality, no library actually needs to. Technology is a tool to be used to meet a library's needs. In much the same way, the library's staff members, collections, and facilities are also resources available to meet the library's needs. For any initiative, the key is to find the right solution to fill a particular need and integrate it into the library environment.

Technology can often improve and streamline library service. However, implementing technology projects smoothly is a challenge in many libraries. As technology evolves so quickly, it is difficult enough to keep up with the changes, let alone successfully incorporate a new system into the library. Whether the project is redesigning a website, installing a print management system, or upgrading staff computers, there are common strategies that can maximize the success of the project and minimize unanticipated hiccups. These strategies can help libraries effectively implement a new technology system of any size in any environment.

If you would like to use your library's limited funds for technology as efficiently as possible, read on to learn the strategies that can optimize your results with any technology project that you undertake.

## Endnotes

1. Federal Communications Commission, "The Digital TV Transition: What You Need to Know About DTV," www.dtv.gov (accessed September 14, 2010).

2. Mary Madden, "State of the Internet 2009: Pew Internet Project Findings and Implications for Libraries," Pew Internet & American Life Project, October 2, 2009, www.pewinternet.org/Presentations/2009/36—State-of-the-Internet-2009—Pew-Internet-Project-Findings-and-Implications-for-Libraries.aspx (accessed November 16, 2010).

3. Pew Internet & American Life Project Tracking Surveys (March 2000–September 2009), "Online Activities, 2000-2009," Pew Internet & American Life Project, December 4, 2009, www.pewinternet.org/Trend-Data/Online-Activities-2000 2009.aspx (accessed January 14, 2010).

4. Denise M. Davis, "The Condition of U.S. Libraries: Trends, 1999–2009," American Library Association, December 2009, www.ala.org/ala/research/initiatives/Condition_of_Libraries_1999.20.pdf (accessed January 14, 2010).

# Chapter 1

# Identify the Library's Needs

Technology projects are successful in libraries when they provide a solution for a need, not just because the library staff wants to experiment with new technology. Yet, many libraries fall into the trap of creating a project just so they can take advantage of the latest high-tech gadget available on the market. These types of projects tend to fizzle and die. They may be cool enough to last for a short while, but if there is no driving need, the technology will end up unused or under-used, and the funds invested in the project are no longer available for a more sustainable endeavor.

Has your library ever implemented some popular technology, only to spend more time—and money—promoting it and explaining it to your customers and/or staff than actually using it? That is a sure sign that it was a bad fit for your community. Technology should never be forced upon your staff or customers. It should be part of a solution that is in the right place at the right time to meet your library's needs.

Sometimes even when technology projects are implemented in libraries to meet a need, the outcome is not as successful as the staff initially predicted. Perhaps the solution was not the best fit for the need, the project was not carefully planned, or the implementation team chose shortcuts that overlooked critical steps along the way. The road to success begins with careful planning.

## Technology Plans

Proper planning and prioritization is critical to meeting the technological demands of library users successfully. All libraries should create and maintain a technology plan. Are you groaning already? Has "write a technology plan" been on your list of things to do for a long time, but you have just never gotten around to it? I know the feeling. Planning takes time, and you never have time to plan because you are too busy doing other work, right? There is an ancient proverb whose original author is unknown, but the words carry a powerful truth: "He who fails to plan, plans to fail." So take the time to write the plan if you want to be successful.

Do you need more motivation? Does your library file for E-Rate funding? If not, or if you do not know what E-Rate is, I encourage you to explore it. E-Rate is a great opportunity for schools and libraries to receive funding assistance for telecommunication and internet services.[1] However, one of the filing requirements is that you have an approved technology plan. Perhaps you are saying, "I know, and since we do not have a technology plan, we do not file for E-Rate." In that case, you are missing out on some possible funding assistance. The details of that program will not be covered in this book. Nonetheless, this is yet another organization encouraging all libraries to plan and therefore to succeed.

If your library does not have a current technology plan, there are many resources available to assist you in creating or updating one. The American Library Association (ALA) has put together a guide called *Technology for Results,*[2] which describes how to create a technology plan for your library. In addition, the online resource WebJunction has a variety of resources available to assist with the planning process, including free software called TechAtlas.[3] I encourage all readers to explore these and other resources more fully, if you do not already have a tech plan in place or if you want to improve your existing one.

## Plan Components

While this chapter will not go into the details of writing your technology plan, I do want to highlight the basics. Most technology plans should cover a three-year period. With the rate that technology changes, it is sometimes difficult to plan three years ahead. Before you actually implement anything in your plan, you will want to review whether the project is still suitable for your library's needs. However, it is important to look three years down the road and incorporate goals to strive for.

The major components of your technology plan should include:

1. Your library's mission

2. Clear goals and realistic strategies for using technology to improve services in your library (with measurable milestones)

3. Staff development plan to train employees in how to use the technology

4. Assessment/inventory of current services, hardware, and software

5. Budget

6. Evaluation

You will find a sample technology plan included as Appendix A of this book for your review. You are welcome to use it as a guideline for your own library's technology plan. This is the plan that I use at my library. Yours certainly does not have to look like mine; it should include the major components, but it will reflect your community and your library's needs.

If you do not have a current technology plan for your library, take time to write one. Include key decision makers at your library in the process. The plan should identify needs in all departments of the library and accurately reflect the library's technology initiatives. Technology needs exist for both library customers and library staff. Take a look at the entire picture and prioritize what needs to be done. With a good plan, many things are possible.

The technology plan focuses on the goals and the objectives for meeting those goals. Sometimes it can include details about specific solutions to help meet those goals. Many technology plans define the needs (in terms of goals and objectives) but omit the details, leaving them up to the project implementation team to identify. This strategy provides the most flexibility to adapt to the ever-changing technology.

Once your technology plan is complete, it becomes your guide for the three-year period. The projects you will implement are outlined in your plan. You may need to upgrade computers, redesign your website, install new security cameras, or migrate to a new integrated library system. No matter what the project is, there is a time and a place specified in your plan to do the investigation and implementation.

Because technology changes so frequently, unanticipated needs may come up, and some defined needs may fade away or be replaced by higher priorities. Therefore, your plan is an outline and should be somewhat flexible. It serves as a guideline and gives you a structure that you can use to implement technology projects that improve library services.

# Info City, USA

Throughout this book, we are going to walk along with a fictional library staff, as its members go through the process of implementing a technology solution for their customers. Allow me to introduce them to you. Once upon a time, there was a village in a state in America. The village's name is Info City. About 62,000 people live in Info City and enjoy visiting their very own public library. The Info City Public Library (ICPL) provides a varied collection of materials, access to the internet, programs for residents of all ages, and much more. ICPL staff strive to maintain a high level of customer service and support for their customers' information needs.

Your library, like ICPL, has a technology need (likely many needs). Identify the one that is the current priority for your library, based on the timeline in your plan, and you are ready to move forward.

# Endnotes

1. Universal Service Administrative Company, Schools and Libraries Program of the Universal Service Fund, www.usac.org/sl (accessed August 3, 2009).

2. Diane Mayo, *Technology for Results: Developing Service-Based Plans* (Chicago: ALA Editions, 2005).

3. WebJunction, TechAtlas for Libraries, webjunction.techatlas.org (accessed October 29, 2009).

# Chapter 2

# Project Teams and Initial Research

With a technology plan in hand, a library has a clear structure for initiating new projects. The process will vary for each library environment, but the general practice will look something like this: A person in authority (such as the library director) identifies the need for a new project, often from following the goals and objectives in the technology plan. He meets with his management team to initiate and prioritize the project. Together, they discuss the goals and objectives that they will strive to accomplish. They work collaboratively to define the need, draft the expected outcomes, and clearly spell out any requirements. The project is then handed off to the capable hands of the project manager to identify all of the details and work through the implementation.

## Build Your Project Team

Creating a successful project team begins with selecting the right person as the project manager. In some cases, this is the person whose work will be most directly affected by the new system. For other projects, someone in an authoritative role at the library is put in charge because she has the responsibility and influence needed to get the project done. Alternatively, the project manager is the one who is the most knowledgeable about the project and the possible solutions. The project manager must be someone who is able to make the hard decisions and keep the project on track.

After the project is initiated, defined, and assigned, the project manager must carefully craft her team to include the key stakeholders in the project. The size and makeup of the team will depend on the scope of the project. For a project that will affect the entire library, it is helpful to have a representative from each library department on the team. This representative could be responsible for communicating the progress of the project back to his respective department. If the project will only affect one specific library department, then the team will likely be smaller and include members from that specific department.

Even if the project will only affect one department, it will be important to let the rest of the library staff know what is going on, perhaps once at the onset of the project and then again at the end of implementation. I have often found in libraries that communication about library projects to all staff members is a sizable challenge. However, without it, misinformation is often shared with others (including library customers), and libraries, of all places, should be a source of authoritative information.

When selecting team members, it is important to recognize that the team members do not always have to be the department heads, managers, or supervisors. In fact, it can be helpful to include hourly staff or specialized staff on your project team (when appropriate) as their perspective is often fresh and insightful.

An important note about technology project teams: Include both technical and nontechnical staff on your project team in some way from the beginning. IT staff members in libraries can often be one of two extremes: "typical IT guys" who do not understand libraries, or library staff members who have an aptitude for technology but may not have sufficient background to handle the details. In some libraries, the "typical IT guys" are not even on the regular payroll at the library, but rather they are contracted from an external company when needed or pulled from the city's or university's IT department. In either case, it is important to include people in the discussion who have expertise in both areas and the ability to bridge the gap. In addition, be sure you include people who can communicate the technical details of the project to the less technical staff at the library. Communication will be critical during the project planning and implementation, and you need to ensure that everyone understands the plan in the same way when making decisions. If you are lucky enough to have talented IT staff who truly understand the needs of libraries, it is still critical to include other staff members in the process to gain their perspective and buy in, which will improve the probability of success.

How big should your project team be? That really depends on the scope of the work. Many project management books will tell you to include five to seven people on any project team. More than that and you end up with too many opinions; fewer than that and you might be missing someone important. However, that is just a basic guideline. If your project involves highly technical work, then the IT staff (which may only be one or two people) could be the only people involved in the implementation. However, no matter how big or small the team is, as long as you have the key stakeholders involved, you are moving in the right direction.

OK. So you have a project defined. You have a project manager, and you have a team. Now what? Well, now the fun begins: It is time to meet!

# Meetings

Now I'm sure many of you are smirking. Isn't that what libraries are really good at? Creating committees (project teams) and having long meetings where nothing is accomplished? It does happen that way in many libraries and in other organizations as well. My goal here is to share with you ways to avoid the unproductive meeting spiral.

Meetings are important—but they have to serve a purpose. Let me make an important distinction between a project team, which is what this book covers, and a committee: A project team has a specific purpose—to implement a project. Once the project is implemented, your team members will need to ask themselves, does this team still have a purpose? If it does (such as ongoing maintenance on the project, updates, etc.), then the team may want to continue to meet as there will be work to do. If it does not, then the team can safely disband, knowing that another team will be formed in the future when another project needs to be implemented.

I have seen libraries create committees for every purpose under the sun. And libraries like to create catchy names for their committees (I was once a member of NAG, the Novi Automation Group). But a committee too often serves no productive purpose. It probably had a purpose at one point, perhaps to implement a project. Or maybe it is just a group of people who like to touch base once a month, using meetings as a communication tool.

Meetings are important communication tools ... when there is information to share. However, I firmly believe that a committee, a group of people not currently working on any given project, does not need to create meetings for the sake of meetings. Have you ever attended a meeting where there was no agenda? Or where there was an extremely short and vague agenda? Perhaps you have tried to run a meeting where you did not really have anything to say except, "Well, it's the second Thursday of the month, so we better get together again." I have. Guilty on both counts, actually. And it is not surprising that I found those experiences to be a fruitless way to spend time. The meetings I describe and encourage throughout this book serve the purpose of moving a project forward toward its completion. Project teams need scheduled meetings with agendas and action items. There are more ideas ahead, and we will discuss these tools and others that project teams find useful. For now, to get started, plan your first team meeting.

# Sample Meeting Agenda

The project manager sets up a meeting time and location and invites all the team members. What is on the agenda for this first meeting? (Remember that I said these meetings will have agendas?)

Introduction and Brainstorm

1. Introduce the team members. If the project includes staff members from different departments, go around the table and have everyone introduce themselves. Once each team member has been introduced, use a brief icebreaker to create a sense of collaboration. It could be something as simple as asking each person to share something about themselves that the others in the room do not already know (favorite hobby, pet, sports team, etc.). The cohesiveness of the team will be important to the success of the project. This initial time provides a chance to see your teammates as people who have interests beyond the job they do at your library.

2. Discuss the origin of and need for the project. Your team will need to understand why the project is important and why they may even find it exciting and interesting. Talk with your project team about the library's need and how this project aims to find a solution that will meet that need. Reinforce that each team member is critical to the success of the project. Project managers (or supervisors in general) often have a tendency to hold back some information from their team members. Libraries do enforce a strong value in protecting the privacy of their staff and customers, which may lead to withholding information of that nature. However, when you are implementing a new project, sharing information among team members will encourage participation and foster understanding.

3. Define the expected outcomes for the project. In addition to sharing the need for the project, it is important to outline the expected outcomes of the project from the very beginning. These include the expectations that were defined by the management team when the project was assigned. In addition, the project manager will likely have

expectations of his team members specifically. These also need to be clearly defined at this initial meeting. This project definition will also set the tone for the extent of the project.

4. Outline the requirements for the project. Remember that at this point, no solution has been determined yet, but any solution will need to fulfill certain project requirements. Some requirements are established by the management team when the project is assigned. Other requirements will become more defined as the project begins to take shape.

5. Open the floor for general discussion of the project. At this point in the meeting, it is time to welcome and encourage comments from your team members. These could be general thoughts about the project, reactions to the expectations or requirements, or even questions about what has been said so far. Try to get a sense from the team members as to their overall interest and excitement for the project. If you have some naysayers on your team, make a note to speak with them individually about their concerns. Try to maintain a positive tone in the conversation, and mediate the discussion so that anyone who wants to has a chance to share.

6. Brainstorm high-level ideas of solutions to meet the need. Transition the conversation from open discussion to actual brainstorming of ideas. Remind the team that brainstorming does not include judgment on any of the ideas presented. It is an open floor to throw out ideas, which could be actual solutions, general ideas on features to include, or even concerns about the project. This is a good opportunity for the project leader to get a feel for the team. It is important that every member of the team participate in some way. Do not let one team member dominate the conversation, and do not let team members

offer opinions on the ideas of their colleagues. Use a white board or easel to record all of the ideas presented. Be sure to transcribe the ideas to an electronic file after the meeting for future reference.

7. Summarize, make assignments, and define the next steps. After the brainstorming begins to subside and team members seem satisfied that their ideas have been voiced, briefly summarize the ideas on the list. Do not remove any entries from the list at this point. Inform the team of your expectations of them before the next meeting. Everyone should have a task to do so that each person takes part of the responsibility for moving the project along. These tasks are the action items mentioned previously as a useful tool for a successful team. Direct all team members to think further about the project, research any additional ideas, and bring any further suggestions or questions to the next meeting. Finally, set the next meeting date. Ideally, no more than two weeks should pass between meetings at this point in the project, and preferably only one week, in order to build the momentum and keep the project moving along. If you can outline the entire timeline for the project, it is helpful to do so. If that is not possible yet, ask everyone to bring calendars to the next meeting, when you will define the overall project timeline.

First meeting accomplished! The project has officially kicked off, and your team is working toward a new goal. As a general guideline, keep project team meetings to an hour in length, knowing that some might take more and some might take less. But an hour is a good average amount of time for keeping everyone focused on the project at hand. (Providing chocolate as a brain stimulant is typically appreciated as well!)

If you are the project manager, it is your job to transcribe the ideas from the brainstorming session and send them out to the team, along with brief meeting minutes. For future meetings, you can appoint a scribe to take the minutes. If your library has the infrastructure in place, share your notes on an intranet, blog, or wiki, as appropriate. Otherwise, share via email, along with reminders of when the next team meeting will be and what the team should be working on before then.

# Initial Research

Going forward, you will have one or two more team meetings in order to narrow down your list of ideas. (I trust that you can create the appropriate meeting agendas for these future meetings.) Your goal is to identify between four and six possible solutions. Depending on the scope of the project, your team may not be able to list actual solutions but rather will determine specific features that the solution must have and/or potential challenges that the project may present.

In order to do this, the team members will need to do some initial research to ensure that everyone understands the possibilities. And luckily, library staff tend to excel at research! Have your team members either pair up or work individually on the research in between the team meetings. Resources abound for gathering information about subjects that are new to us. We can look online to get started. We can search through the library literature and professional and technical journal articles. We will begin to have a better understanding of different ways to accomplish our goal.

Do not underestimate the knowledge of your peers. In my experience, library staff members are extremely willing to share information with each other. Post questions on library email lists. Find out how other libraries have solved the types of problems that your library is facing. Did the solution work well? If so, why was it successful? If not, what were the downfalls and what would have made it better? What was required to make the solution work? Keep in mind that each library will undoubtedly have a unique experience

with any project, but the lessons learned by one library can benefit others.

During this research time, team members should compile notes
that they will share with the rest of the team at the next meeting.
The notes should include, but not be limited to: a solid explanation
of how the solution would help the library; the benefits of implementing that type of solution; the challenges the library would face
with that type of solution; and any specific library or organization
that has direct experience with the solution, as they might be a
valuable resource in the future.

# Report Back

These techniques—doing research and taking notes—are additional tools that assist project teams. At the next meeting, team
members will all report back what they learned about possible
solutions, using their notes as a guide. Any questions that cannot be answered should be documented for further research. By
the end of this meeting, each member of the project team
should have a solid understanding of the various types of solutions available. It is very important that all team members are on
the same page before moving on with the project, in order for
the team to work together toward the common goal. You are
working to narrow your list down to a short list of solutions
and/or features, which you will explore in much more detail in
the upcoming chapters.

# Checking In With
# Info City Public Library

At ICPL, the director meets regularly with his department managers to identify project priorities collaboratively. When a new
project is at the top of the priority list, the department managers

and director have an initial discussion to formulate a clear direction for the project. The project is then handed off to the project leader. At ICPL, the IT manager leads the projects that are defined in the technology plan.

The technology plan for ICPL states that the library should "provide fair access to computer technology to meet customer needs." The impetus behind this goal in ICPL's technology plan is that its library does not have enough computers for everyone in the community who needs to use one. The library's public computers are self-managed on a first-come, first-served basis, but the staff hears many complaints from customers who say they are never able to use a computer because all the stations are always in use by others. The library board is being pressured to buy more computers, but there is dissension about how many computers are needed, and limited funds are in the budget. So the library needs to find a way to better manage the demand for public computing.

After a project discussion where the details are clarified, the director of ICPL hands off the project to the IT manager to implement. The IT manager identifies four staff members from the public service departments in the library, as well as an additional IT staff member, to make up her team. The team initially meets three times. At the first meeting, they brainstorm and come up with many ideas, including adding more computers, reassigning staff to manage the computers, using a software solution to help manage computer sessions and/or printing, and many more. They then do additional research to understand what options are available to them and discuss the options as a team in their second meeting.

They narrow down these ideas down to this shorter list of key features needed to resolve the problem:

- More computers would help but not solve the problem.

- Staff do not have enough time to manage the equipment, so a system is needed that is generally self-service.

- The system should handle both computer management and print management.

- For computer management:

  - Staff members need to be able to define different rules for different areas of the library.

  - Filtering should be supported at various levels.

  - Customers should be allowed to stay on a computer as long as no one else is waiting.

  - Customers must log in with a library card and be in good standing.

  - Guests who are not eligible for a library card should be allowed to use a computer but with a shorter time session than a library cardholder.

  - Users must accept the library's Internet Policy before gaining access to the computer.

- For print management:

  - The system must allow the library to set different prices for black and white and color printing.

  - The system should allow customers to pay for printouts by cash, credit card, or money deposited to a personal printing account.

  - Printing should be allowed from the wireless network.

  - Use of a print release station is preferred.

  - Customers should be able to pick up their print jobs at any public print release station.

These are the features that the team will explore in more depth in the next steps.

# Chapter 3

# Research Further and Identify Vendors

With the short list of important features in hand, it is time for more in-depth research and information gathering. The research will need to determine which solutions are available to meet the specific needs defined by the project. The team will need to investigate the available solutions and determine how well they provide the detailed features on the short list. The team members will need at least two or three weeks to do their research. The project manager should also do her own research on all of the ideas, which at the minimum should be enough to help explain or add to what the team members find in order to aid the discussion.

This additional investigation can be accomplished with some of the same methods as the first round of research (online resources, library literature, and colleagues). In addition, team members should look even further and make contact directly with vendors. If the timing aligns with an upcoming conference, visit the exhibit hall at the conference and speak directly to vendors. Find out how specific solutions work and what they will do for your library. View demonstrations of solutions to get a solid understanding of how they work. If visiting a vendor or conference is not possible, call vendors and ask about online demonstrations or short-term trials. Visit nearby libraries that are using the system and see how it works for them.

Some team members should focus on the technical specifications while others should examine the less tangible features. Ask hard questions and seek honest answers. Investigate the vendor's reputation and commitment to customer service. Get references. Vendors should always be able to provide you with names and contact information for other libraries that use their technology. Contact those libraries and talk with them about their experiences, both with the product(s) and with the company. Go beyond the list that the vendor provides and ask around on library lists. In my experience, library staff members are willing to share their honest experiences with others. This is particularly helpful if you do not know what to ask the vendor directly. If you are venturing into unknown territory, ask others what pitfalls they encountered and how they were handled by the vendor. If the product is not supported by a specific vendor (such as in an open source system), find out what support would be available to your library if the solution was chosen for implementation.

As with the first round of research, each team member should collect notes to share with the full project team. At the next team meeting, go around the table again and let each person report. See which solutions were investigated by multiple team members and whether their findings were similar or different. Are there any discrepancies in what was discovered? Many times, the more questions you ask, the more questions you have. Do further questions need to be asked? Pull out your agreed-upon feature list—does it need to be revised?

# Document the Requirements

The final step at this stage is to put into writing a detailed list of desired features for your project. Throughout your team's research, you have gathered a great deal of information, analyzed it, and made some important decisions. You have identified the features that take priority in your desired solution, as well as the functionality that is critical to your project's success. Take the time to write it all down. In addition, document the possible vendors and/or solutions identified by the team. This document will become the master definition of the project's requirements and will enable the team to stay focused and work cohesively.

# Request for Proposal

Depending on your library, you may be required to issue a request for proposal (RFP). This is a formal document that describes the library's project and asks vendors to bid on the project. The RFP must include a clear set of feature requirements, with as much detail as possible. A well-structured RFP will greatly increase the likelihood that the proposals submitted will be easier to evaluate and provide an apples-to-apples comparison for your team. If you have completed the documentation of your project requirements, it will translate directly to the list of requirements in your RFP.

So how do you write an RFP? There are a variety of resources available to assist you. First, ask your colleagues if anyone has written an RFP similar to the one you need, as theirs may serve as a model for your own. Why reinvent the wheel? Second, look online for assistance. Online resources at WebJunction[1] and TechSoup[2] include articles created for libraries about writing an RFP. There are even books about how to write an RFP. Each RFP will vary depending on the project and the library environment. But if you define the requirements of your project as clearly as possible, you should receive some viable proposals.

A sample RFP is included as Appendix B. It is an RFP for a digital security camera system, so the details are specific to that project and technology. However, note that this RFP includes a great deal of technical specifications, identified clearly to narrow the scope of the responses. The more explicit you are in your RFP, the more precise your responses will be.

Armed with the team's completed document that defines the required features, the project manager is tasked with writing the RFP. Include all contact information for any questions the vendor may have and provide a clear due date. Generally, you want to allow two to four weeks from the time your vendors receive your RFP to the date the responses are due to be returned to you. When completed, the RFP should be sent out to all the vendors identified by the team as good candidates for providing a viable solution that meets your library's needs. If you want to broaden the search, you can also post the RFP where other possible vendors may see it. You may be contacted by potential vendors to answer questions as they create their proposals, but generally once the RFP is sent out, you will find that you have a little time to breathe in the project plan as the vendors prepare their responses. When you receive proposal responses, date them so you know when you received them and keep them sealed until the final deadline day and time arrives, at which time you may want to hold a public bid opening, depending on your community.

# No RFP Required

If your library, city, university, or other governing body does not require a formal RFP process, then you may be able to find a vendor on your own, based on your team's research. Some projects are straightforward enough that an RFP is not necessary to locate the best solution. Perhaps the desired solution is specialized and only one vendor can provide what you need. Or perhaps the vendor is not a company you hire or even a system you purchase but rather an open source or free system. Some libraries have internal resources available to build the optimal solution. Even in these cases, defining your desired solution and clearly listing the required features ensures that the outcome will match the original concept. So take the time to write it out—it will pay off down the road.

If a project team is the group making the recommendation without an RFP process, the team will need ample time for research and/or discussion before reaching consensus on which solution to implement. In addition, the team should be sure to set up demonstrations of the various solutions in order to truly see how the systems work. As the team members work through their research, they should document each possible solution to have a reference point for analysis. List each solution and the important features of the system. Include any items that are distinctive or could possibly differentiate one solution from another. After all, this is what the vendors responding to an RFP will do. The team's own documentation will then be the resource for analysis.

# Reviews, Ratings, and Recommendations

Once the research is completed by the team and/or the proposals are returned by the vendors, another difficult task is at hand. The team must carefully review and analyze the options. Each team member should individually assess each proposal, and each team member should be vigilant and impartial.

It is much like judging a competition. When the judges at the Olympics evaluate athletic performances, they watch closely and rate each athlete on how well he performs when compared against the requirements. Similarly, the team members should review each vendor and compare them against the requirements. Did you forget about the requirements? That is the list of features that your project team has prioritized as most important to the success of your project.

The easiest way to provide a fair assessment of the vendors is to use a review tool. The project manager should design a review tool that each team member can fill out for each proposal. Creating the review tool is simple. Pull out that list of requirements and provide a way to rate how well each vendor meets each requirement. Some of the requirements may be weighted more heavily than others. And in addition to the functional requirements, be sure to include appropriate requirements that reflect the importance of the relationship with the vendor, cost, and the overall completeness of the proposal.

A sample review tool is included as Appendix C. For continuity, this is a review tool that was used with the RFP responses received for the security camera project, the sample RFP included in Appendix B. Note that the criteria in the review allow for weighted comparisons of the various proposals.

Allow enough time for each team member to complete the review tool for each vendor and send the completed review to the project manager to compile. Once the compilation is assembled, share it with all the team members and schedule your next team meeting within a week. Let team members know that they need to review the compilation and come to the meeting ready to discuss their options.

# Decisions, Decisions

The next meeting may be a difficult one, because team members may have differing opinions about the quality of the proposals received and which solution should be chosen. Begin with an overview of the assembled reviews. Identify the trends among the proposals. Based purely on the rating scale itself, I would expect a couple of vendors to bubble to the surface while others may drop out of consideration. Discuss the results openly and determine if there is significant disagreement. It is critical to get input from each team member as to which direction they feel is the best one for the library and why.

This discussion must be focused on the current need that the team is addressing. Any concerns about how the library used to do things or why the staff will never be able to learn something new must be dismissed from the conversation unless these issues are discussed constructively.

If nothing can be decided or if consensus becomes difficult, this process may take more than one team meeting, and the team may need to gather more information. But the team needs to be in agreement before moving forward. If there is serious dissension among the team members, air the reasons honestly. Everyone's input is valuable.

# Spotlight: Managing Change

Shortly after I started working at the Rochester Hills Public Library in Michigan, the web team was working to redesign the library website. The web team had been using Microsoft FrontPage to modify static HTML pages. Each person on the team was assigned certain pages that she was responsible for. This structure was fairly common in libraries when web development began, and it worked for them. They were comfortable with it. When I suggested going to a content management system called Joomla, some of the team members were justifiably concerned. They understood that they needed to make the website easier to manage and were willing to explore something new. But Joomla was quite different: Would they be able to do all the things they needed to with it?

The decision to implement Joomla was not a team decision at the time, but I did my best to train the staff on the software and provide access to help resources. I also had one of my IT staff members (who is the library's Joomla expert) available for initial training sessions and one-on-one assistance throughout the process.

The concerns of the web team were valid and needed to be addressed in order for the project to be successful. Throughout the project, the team struggled at times to get Joomla to display the web content as they envisioned it. However, they also learned a number of new things along the way, and the library's new website launched on June 1, 2008. Even the web team members who were originally very hesitant about Joomla are now happy with the new site and continue to learn more about Joomla all the time. In 2009, the library also used Joomla to develop its staff intranet website, so many more staff members have learned how the software works, and Joomla has proven to be a successful tool in the library.

The point of this story is not the happily-ever-after tale that it appears to be. There were growing pains along the way for the library. However, the important part of the story is how the initial concerns were addressed. I was not the Joomla expert, but I led the project. At the time, I pushed the solution through because I knew the advantages of the software would be very helpful in the future, and I was confident that it would work well. I did not brush the staff concerns under the rug, but I also did not necessarily acknowledge them to the extent that the staff might have wanted.

It is important that the team members feel that they are working together, but making everyone equally happy is not always possible. So when various solutions are discussed at this point in the process, concerns will be voiced about the challenges that come with their implementation. No doubt each concern will be valid. Some concerns will be technical or functional in nature; those are real and could affect the outcome of the project. Others are more emotional, arising where the staff is internally adapting to the change; those are also real to the team members, but a productive way to handle them is by acknowledging the concern and then flooding the team with sincere confidence in the outcome of the project.

Much success is realized through confidence, not empty confidence, but sincere belief, supported by a real plan for achievement. If the concerns of your team members give rise to valid reasons that the project plan needs more attention, acknowledge them and create a solution in the plan that leads to success. True belief in yourself and your team will go a very long way during the implementation of your project.

When I took my first professional job in a library, my first boss told me that we had to get the "buy in" of my colleagues in order to move forward with a project. I understood what she meant at the time, and her intention was good. However, I also believe that some library staff spend a great deal of time in committee meetings trying to get everyone else to buy in to their idea or to move forward through implementing a project. When a team is implementing a new solution, the team has to have the same intention: moving forward. Therefore, consensus is critical. However, project managers can spend hours and hours trying to make the entire team happy about the decisions, and that may not always be possible. More importantly, it is possible to acknowledge the expressed concerns of team members, address those that will truly affect the outcome, and respond to the rest with sincere confidence that a successful outcome will be achieved.

## Consensus

Remember, consensus is critical at this juncture. Once the team agrees on a solution, everything progresses and there is no looking back during implementation. Address concerns and instill confidence in success. When consensus is reached, celebrate this milestone as a team.

## Checking In With Info City Public Library

The project team at ICPL has created its initial list of features. The members are looking for solutions for computer and print management and specifically solutions that meet their requirements. What computer and print management systems are available? Do they have the features that the team has identified? How flexible are they? And will they fit well in the library environment?

The team members do some further research into the available solutions for computer and print management. They already know about some of the vendors, but they discover others during their research. They identify a total of eight vendors that offer solutions that might work for the library. In addition, their research allows the team members to clarify their requirements and prioritize the functionality that their library needs. They work together to document their requirements as clearly as possible.

ICPL requires the use of an RFP when making large purchases. Therefore, the project manager has to create an RFP that outlines the required features as defined by the team. The RFP is sent out to the eight identified vendors. While awaiting the responses, the project manager is a bit relieved to find some quiet time. She creates the review tool for her team members, based on their documented requirements, and provides it to the team. They will need to use it to review each vendor response received.

Once the RFP due date arrives, the team members are fully engaged in the project once again. ICPL has received five responses before the deadline: CASSIE, Comprise, EnvisionWare, Librarica, and Pharos. The project team members use the review tool to compare and contrast the responses from the different vendors. The criteria are weighted in terms of priority of what is most important to their library environment.

After weighing the features and proposals from the vendors, and much discussion about the options, the team comes to a consensus that it would like to work with EnvisionWare for a computer and print management system. And they celebrate this milestone with a team dinner at the local pub!

## Endnotes

1. WebJunction, "Buying Technology," www.webjunction.org/buying-technology (accessed December 2, 2010).
2. TechSoup for Libraries, "Buying and Deploying Technology," www.techsoupforlibraries.org/cookbook-3/buying-and-deploying-technology (accessed December 2, 2010).

# Chapter 4

# Contract With a Vendor

You and your team have finally decided which solution you will implement to meet the current library need. If you are purchasing a solution from a vendor who will be assisting with the implementation, the project manager should be the main contact for working out the details of the contract with the vendor. A single point of contact is important for the project's success, as it encourages reliable communication and decision making.

However, a single point of contact does not mean a single point of input. The project manager's task at this point is to write up a recommendation to the person of authority (whoever initiated the project and assigned the project manager—at ICPL, it is the library director). The recommendation should outline the chosen solution and vendor for the project. A well-documented recommendation will demonstrate the support of all the team members and give all team members credit for their work on the project. The recommendation should detail both the research completed and the reasons for the recommended solution.

A sample recommendation letter is included as Appendix D. Once again, this is related to the security camera project (the sample RFP and review tool included as well in Appendices B and C). In this case, the recommendation is addressed to the library director and library board. It outlines the highlights of the various proposals received. It includes a recommendation of the preferred vendor's solution and the criteria that make the preferred system the best fit for the library. These criteria will vary for each library, based on local policies and priorities.

Once the project manager has drafted the recommendation, she should set up a quick team meeting for a final review of the recommendation and to provide time for each team member to sign the recommendation letter. Finally, the recommendation should be signed by the project manager and taken to the person of authority for further review or approval.

In some libraries, whenever money is spent or contracts are signed, the library board must approve the purchase and/or contract with a vendor. In others, the approval must come from a purchasing department, city council, or other realm of the organization. In these larger organizations where the structure requires channels of approval, the recommendation from the project team becomes increasingly important. But each library is different, and these details should be tailored to fit your library's needs.

# Finalize the Details

Once the recommendation has been approved by the person in authority, the project manager can begin to work directly with the vendor on the details of the contract and an initial plan for implementation. The term *vendor* here does not necessarily have to refer to an outside company. In the case of an open source solution or a project to be implemented entirely in-house, there may not be a contract to sign, but there will be a commitment made to implementing the project with certain tools. It is critical at this stage in the process to define how these tools will be used for your library's project. The project manager must ensure that the library and the vendor have the same understanding of the desired solution while building a working relationship.

These initial conversations will undoubtedly set the stage for future interactions. It is important for the library's project manager to be prepared and organized, so the vendor holds the library in high regard. At the same time, it is vital for the library project manager to get a good sense of how the vendor responds. Ideally by this point, the library staff feels a sense of trust in the vendor, but until the work begins, it is hard to know exactly what to expect. If any red flags are raised during these initial conversations, it is critical to address your concerns before it is too late.

Ask all of your questions. Make sure that you understand the answers and that there are no gray areas. Define your expectations and ask the vendor to define his. If there are special conditions that you and the vendor have agreed on (specific functionality, custom configuration, etc.), insist that they are put in writing so that everyone knows what is to be done. Determine a timeline: When will implementation start and how long should it take? What will the process be? What will the library be responsible for and what will the vendor provide?

When the vendor sends you paperwork to sign, be sure that you fully understand everything on it. Contracts, purchase orders, and even invoices often contain information and legalese that the nonsalesperson cannot understand. (I'd even bet that not all salespeople understand them entirely!) This is true in all industries, not just technology or libraries. In fact, it's worse in other industries sometimes.

# Details Hidden in the Paperwork

I recently purchased a new car. In general, I detest going to car dealerships. Conventionally, purchasing a new car involves haggling with a salesperson, and stereotypically, a salesperson walks all over a female customer, assuming she has no idea what she is doing. Even though I am a modern and confident woman, this type of environment is one I avoid whenever possible. Nonetheless, I did my homework ahead of time, and I knew what I wanted, so I walked into a dealership and spoke to a salesperson. I told him what I wanted and what I had to trade. I could tell he was trying to find a balance between getting on my good side and working to seal the deal. After a while, we reached an agreement that I was happy with, so I agreed to a purchase.

When it was time to finalize the paperwork, I met with the finance manager at the dealership, where I faced a plethora of papers to sign: new purchase, trade-in, financing, warranty, etc. With each one, I took a moment to read what I was signing and ask a few questions, but like most people, I did not want to read every line of each document. However, it was not until I was looking over the actual documents that I became aware of certain details that were "stretched" by the salesperson in order to get my approval.

He had told me that they were going to "wipe away" what was owed on my current vehicle in the trade. Well, they were, but not because they were giving me full credit—rather, they were taking the excess owed and tying it into this new loan. My salesperson had also told me they were offering a great low interest rate. Well, they were, but not on the vehicle I was purchasing. I could have changed my mind on the sale, but after some discussions with the finance manager, I was satisfied with how the deal turned out. So I was able to drive home in my new car that day.

The lesson in this story is that the truth sometimes hides in the verbal messages, but it cannot be entirely concealed when the details are spelled out on paper. If you do not understand what the paperwork says or means, you have a responsibility to ask. You undoubtedly have a library board, library director, city manager, or at least a higher level boss you report to who will hold you responsible for your vendor contracts. Ensure that what you are buying is what you ordered.

Do the best you can. Inevitably you will miss something. You will misunderstand something. When you actually begin implementation, you will discover that something is not quite as you expected. And that is OK. Your project can (and will) still be successful as you work through any unexpected details. But the more you can clarify up front, the better off you will be.

Throughout this time, you are building a relationship with your vendor, which will be critical to the success of your implementation. Build a relationship with someone you trust, someone who understands your needs, someone you are willing and able to work with closely. Once the contract is signed, it is difficult to go backward.

## Spotlight: The Truth About Salespeople

At this point, vendors are working to get your business. They are selling you on a solution. You are talking to salespeople. And no doubt, you have a certain sense of how salespeople can behave. Salespeople did not get a reputation for "talking a good talk" without reason. Salespeople are likely working for a commission, so some salespeople will tell you whatever you want to hear in order to get the sale. And in some companies, salespeople will sell you on something, but when it comes time to actually implement it, the technical staff will become very frustrated because the salespeople misspoke or overpromised.

This is not unusual. It happens frequently. And it rarely leads to a happy ending when it does. So what do we do about it?

Ask questions. If you do not understand something, ask. And make sure your vendor provides you with an acceptable answer. If you do not get enough information in the response, ask for more information. Ask to speak with a technical staff member at the company. Ask if you can get a free 30-day (or longer) evaluation of the solution before purchasing.

Go back to the references, especially if you do not think you are getting honest answers from your vendor. Discussions with other customers will likely spark new understanding and will shape your own expectations. Do not be shy, as your library staff is depending on you to lead them through an important project. You should feel free to share what you learn about other libraries' experiences with your vendor directly. This tells your vendor that you are doing your homework and you are serious about the success of your library's project.

Do your own research. Your team has already done a lot of research by this point. But if there are new red flags raised during your experience, do more research. You must be absolutely comfortable with the vendor or else the project will not succeed.

Please note that there is another side to this story: Not all salespeople fit the stereotype. Just as not all IT people love *Star Trek*, not all salespeople are only interested in making a deal. There are "good" vendors out there who want to form a mutually beneficial relationship with you. They understand that your success means that you will share your experience with others, which could bring them more business. Some will tell you frankly when they don't have an answer or when their product will not do what you want it to do. These are the precious gems in a mountain of stones. If you find one, or even create one through a good working experience, hang on to it. A positive vendor relationship will go a long way toward building a successful future for both your library and the vendor itself.

# Checking In With Info City Public Library

Our project manager has written up a recommendation for her director to contract with EnvisionWare. Before taking her recommendation to her director, she sets up a meeting with her project team for one final review and to acquire signatures.

Our team declares its approval of the recommendation to work with EnvisionWare, and all team members are listed in support of the decision as it goes to the library director. The director of ICPL is accountable to a library board. Therefore, the final approval needs to be put on the agenda for the next board meeting. After the meeting, the library director reports that the board has approved the recommendation and funding, and the team is authorized to move forward.

Off and running, our project manager first shares this information with the team members via email and requests a team meeting to plan for implementation. Additionally, she reports back to her EnvisionWare salesperson that the decision has been made to move forward with the proposal and requests the plan for the next steps. Her salesperson expresses appreciation and enthusiasm, and he sends over the contract for her to review and sign.

Before getting too far ahead of herself, the project manager also must send letters to the other vendors who sent in proposals to let them know of the library's decision to move forward with another vendor instead. This is standard procedure for the bid process at ICPL. The rejected vendors may request a summary of the bids that were submitted or may question why a different vendor was chosen; these requests are not uncommon and are usually satisfied with some general information.

When our project manager receives the contract draft from EnvisionWare, she reviews the details carefully. At that point, she has questions, as she wants to understand the caveats in the paperwork, so she calls and speaks with her salesperson. Throughout the process thus far, our project manager has been impressed with the professionalism of the EnvisionWare sales team, and their rapport enables an honest discussion about the details. After receiving answers to her questions and finding no hidden surprises, our project manager sees no roadblocks to signing the contract and is excited to move forward.

# Chapter 5

# Plan for Implementation

Certainly you have already begun planning for the new technology by this point, but now the planning kicks into high gear. Returning your signed contract to the vendor is the milestone that moves your project into the implementation phase. Your vendor will likely assign your project to an implementation specialist—a staff member at the company who will guide your library through the planning and implementation process.

## Kick-Off Meeting/Conference Call

Generally, the process begins with a phone call to kick off the project that includes all team members involved in the project, from both the vendor and the library. The purpose of this call is to introduce all the players and talk through the project to ensure that everyone is on the same page. This is a critical step because up until this point, the library has been working with a salesperson at the company. Generally, the salesperson is on the phone call as well to hand off the project to the implementation specialist at the company. All expectations on both sides need to be spelled out. The contract may be reviewed in detail. All questions and concerns can be brought to the table. Additionally, the vendor will outline the steps in the implementation process: what will happen when, what depends on what, and an overall timeline for completion of the project.

Note that this is typically just the first of many calls to your vendor to go over the process. But this one can set the stage for a successful project. So be prepared, follow through, and stay in communication. Whenever you are on the phone with your vendor, have all the information you need in front of you: a copy of the contract, a copy of the requirements from your project team, your calendar, and as much relevant information as you can collect about your library's technology. In addition, it is often helpful to send out an agenda for these calls ahead of time and distribute minutes to the participants afterward. Often vendors will handle these things as part of their project management process. Even if they do, keep your own notes so you know what was discussed, what the action items are, and who is responsible for doing them.

## Spotlight: IT Tools

As you work through calls with the vendor, typically he will go over the configuration for your system, and you will need to provide information about your library's computers, servers, networks, and printers. You will likely need to know the make and model numbers of hardware to verify compatibility, as well as operating systems and versions of software in use.

A well-organized IT department always has an updated inventory of all its equipment, software, and configurations. If you do not, now is as good a time as any to start one. It is an indispensible tool. After all, if you do not know what you have, then you will never know what you need.

If you do have an IT inventory, as you look it over you may well realize that it is not up-to-date. This is also very common. Someone along the line knew it was important to create one, but as time progressed the documentation was pushed to the wayside and never updated. If this is your situation, at least you have a template to work from. But take some time to update it.

As soon as you start implementing new technologies in your library, you will need to make decisions about what you need and how to make it happen. If you start out basing these decisions on false information, your project will likely be delayed down the road while you sort out the problems caused by misinformation.

Another key tool is an IP Planner. I did not have one of these until a consultant introduced me to it. It is a simple spreadsheet that outlines the IP addresses in your network. Much like an equipment and software inventory, it identifies where your network devices live and therefore how they communicate.

Example templates for both an IT Inventory and an IP Planner can be found as Appendix E and Appendix F, respectively.

Some projects can be entirely implemented remotely. Others may be planned and implemented on-site, with your vendor traveling to your library for meetings and implementation. And some may include a combination of the two; for example, planning may take place remotely via conference calls, while actual installation is done in-person by the vendor. Generally, these decisions are determined by the nature of the project, the location of the vendor and the library, and how much the library is able to pay for installation services. For example, projects that involve installation of new hardware, where the library staff is unfamiliar with configuring the devices, are good candidates for on-site installation, if the funding is available. On the other hand, smaller projects that are software-based, handled by a vendor who can setup remote access to the library, might be successfully installed remotely.

Regardless of the nature of the installation, good planning and communication are critical to the project's success. Make sure that you have exchanged contact information with your vendor so you know how to get in touch as needed. Whenever you have information that would benefit other library staff members, be sure to share it with them so they understand what to expect as well.

# Begin the Planning Process

Typically, projects go through a complete planning process before any installation occurs. Either via a phone call or in a meeting, the vendor walks you through all the steps that will happen when the project is implemented. Keep this process documented and accessible, as you will likely want to refer to it throughout the project to ensure that everything is happening on schedule.

There are often steps that need to be taken prior to actual implementation, depending on the nature of the project and the details in your vendor contract. First, if your project requires it, you will need to order new hardware and/or software (as defined in the contract). Be sure this equipment/software is received by the library before the implementation is scheduled to begin.

Second, the system needs to be designed for your library's environment. Consider the following:

- Which computers/servers will the system be installed on?

- Where will the new hardware be placed?

- Do you need to add network drops and/or power outlets to support the new system?

- Do you need to add furniture to support the new system?

- What are the hardware and software requirements for the system? (Any operating system upgrades, memory upgrades, or other software that needs to be installed?)

- Do you have a test box that you can install first to test the functionality before rolling it out to the entire library?

As you work through the planning documentation on paper, you will also be working through any steps that need to be done prior to the implementation itself. If in the planning process, you have determined that certain computers need upgraded software, then you need to complete the upgrades. If you need to add furniture, re-arrange the environment, or install additional power and/or data connections, then those tasks need to be done. In some cases, these pieces may be part of the contract with your vendor. If not, you need to ensure they are completed before scheduling the installation of your new system. Through these planning phone calls and/or meetings and documentation, it is important to specify clearly who is responsible for completing which tasks. If your vendor expects that the library will have specific steps completed prior to the system's implementation, then you need to see to it that they are accomplished. If you expect the vendor to do them, ensure that the vendor understands that and schedules appropriate time to complete them.

Some technology projects require having other related systems unavailable during installation. Will the staff and/or public users at your library be unable to access their usual resources when you are implementing the new system? If so, give them plenty of advance warning and remind them a day or two before implementation is due to begin. Provide signage at the affected computer areas and information for the public by any method that will reach your users: posters and/or fliers in the library, a library newsletter, the library's website, or just around the staff lounge, depending on how far you need to reach. This communication with your users whose access will be interrupted will help pave the way for a smoother installation.

# Pay Attention to the Details

Some of the biggest pitfalls come from miscommunication. Using documentation to clearly outline responsibilities is a concrete way to try to keep everyone on the same page. However, many more pitfalls come from overlooking the details. Often times this happens because the library does not have the expertise to ask all the necessary questions, and unfortunately the vendor frequently forgets steps in the process. Hopefully this book will help fill in some of the blanks, although it cannot possibly cover every step of every project. But here are some general details you should be aware of, based on my past project experiences.

If your new project involves adding new equipment (hardware), be prepared to know:

- Where you are going to put it:
    - Furniture required
    - Physical dimensions and space
- What it needs to plug into:
    - Power
    - Data (the network)
    - Phone line
    - Other equipment
    - All the cables necessary to make the connections
- What needs to plug into it:
    - Mouse
    - Keyboard
    - Monitor
    - Scanner
    - Printer
    - Other accessories
    - All the proper connection adapters as needed

For any head-end/server room equipment, determine any special requirements:

- Will it fit into the rack, and do you have capacity to access it with your KVM (keyboard, video, mouse) switch?

- Does it require extra power support?

- Do you have network capacity for it in your switches?

- Does it have any special cooling needs to prevent overheating?

- Do you have adequate battery capacity to support the new equipment? Most should be plugged into a backup battery unit in case the library loses power; these come in all shapes and sizes.

For any devices that will be connected to your network, consider the following:

- Determine any firewall access that might need to be configured for the device(s).

- If the application requires remote access, ensure that your network will be configured accordingly.

- Determine which IP addresses (internal and/or external) will be used by the device(s).

- Determine which username/passwords and/or network accounts will be used by the device(s) and create them as necessary.

- Know the administrative user name/password needed to add any devices to your network (for your firewall, switches, servers, etc.).

- Support:
  - How long is the warranty and/or maintenance contract on the new hardware?
  - What exactly does the contract or warranty cover?
  - Who do you call/email for help?

If your new project involves adding new software, be prepared to know:

- Prerequisites or dependencies:
  - Other software that must be installed first (or along with the new software) in order for the new software to work
  - Microsoft Windows updates (or other operating system updates)
  - Web browser plug-ins
  - Freely available tools
  - Any software you've previously purchased and are using that will integrate with the new system
  - Any software that must be purchased to work with the new system (will likely be defined by the vendor when the system is proposed but always confirm this)

- Licensing requirements:
  - Always determine what type of licensing you have for the software (both with the new software you purchase as well as any supporting software you may use with the new system).
  - Know how many devices you can install it on.
  - Know what functionality is available in the version of the software that you have licensed.
  - Find out what is available in an upgraded version, likely at a higher cost, and if it is important to your library environment.

- Support:

  - How long is the maintenance contract on the new hardware?

  - Does it include free upgrades, and how would you acquire and install those?

  - Who do you call/email for help?

If you have questions about the hardware and/or software requirements of your new system, be sure to talk to your vendor about it during the planning phases of your project. If there are items that are up to the library to handle and you do not have the expertise to handle them, consider the following:

- Ask the vendor of your new project for assistance.

- Use the IT support resources you usually use for IT work in your library (staff, consultant, etc.).

- Get assistance from trusted colleagues.

Just be sure to get your questions answered, and ensure you have taken care of your responsibilities to the best of your ability, according to the timeline for your new system. If something is not ready, your project will likely be delayed. If you pay for on-site installation of your new system and your project is delayed once they come on-site to implement, additional travel costs may be incurred if the vendor has to return to your library at a later date to complete the project. Alternatively, the vendor may try to complete the installation remotely, which may or may not turn out as well as you hoped. Therefore, it is in your best interest to go through as much as possible ahead of time.

But in all reality, something may still interrupt the original plan. See Chapter 7 for more information, if needed.

# Checking In With Info City Public Library

When we last checked with the ICPL team, our project manager had worked through the details of the contract with EnvisionWare for the new computer and print management solution. You may also recall that our project manager had arranged a team meeting for her project team to reconvene and refocus on the project. She has now received the date and time for the initial conference call with EnvisionWare, so she wants to get the team organized.

## Team Meeting Time

Upon gathering for the team meeting, our project manager shares the important elements of the contract to remind the team of the scope of the project and get everyone back on the same page. The team members have been on hold somewhat while the project manager was working through the approval and contract process. So reviewing the process and decisions thus far helps refocus the team on where the project is headed.

Additionally, this meeting agenda includes an opportunity for all team members to ask questions and create a list of items to take to the first call with EnvisionWare. As the entire team is invited to this call, this meeting is a good time to let all team members voice their questions and/or concerns about the project. The youth librarian on the ICPL team is interested in understanding how the library's filtering software will be integrated with the computer management software. A circulation staff member wants to understand what will happen when a new customer gets a library card and how the card will work with the computer management software. Another librarian wants to understand better how customers will be able to pick up printouts at any of ICPL's public printers. He also wants to hear more about how guest passes will work. The IT staff member wants to know the exact requirements for the management software so he can ensure IT has all the prerequisites and space needed for installation. These issues, and all others, are compiled into a list to be discussed with EnvisionWare during the conference call.

The project manager also uses time at this meeting to discuss internal logistics for the project implementation. She shares that all team members are welcome to this first call with EnvisionWare and that they will be apprised of all future calls and receive summary minutes of calls, as well as all information pertaining to the progress of the project. However, she notes that it may not be necessary for all team members to attend every subsequent call during the planning process. Some calls will likely address policies, which is where the team's input is valuable. Other calls may address technical details and thus really need to involve only the IT staff. It is important to recognize that including all team members in decisions outside their area of influence is unnecessary and may actually complicate the project further.

At this point, the project manager discusses with the team to what extent its members would like to be involved. One librarian requests to stay involved with all the calls, insofar as his schedule permits. A few others admit that they are happy to bow out of the more technical decisions and will be satisfied with summary information until more actions are required that specifically affect their departments. Knowing that the implementation process is yet to be determined, the team now has some flexibility in its involvement through the planning process. However, it will be all the more critical for our project manager to stay in communication with her team members throughout the planning stages as decisions are made.

This team meeting concludes with a reminder of the date and time for the upcoming call with EnvisionWare and the understanding that future full-team meetings will be scheduled as needed prior to the on-site implementation.

As a follow-up to the team meeting, our project manager sends out a summary of the questions for EnvisionWare and an outline of future logistics. These email summaries are an important part of documenting the process for all involved.

## Team Kick-Off Conference Call

Our project team gathers in the conference room at the appointed time and date and dials into the conference call with the EnvisionWare team. As anticipated, the project salesperson leads the call and introduces the new implementation specialist. The team learns that this call's agenda is to make introductions and briefly go over the project timeline, but any details will be covered in the next call. Though it is not entirely a waste to have the entire team on the call, the project manager requests that agendas for future calls be sent out ahead of time, so that only the team members involved need to be present, and others can use the time for other projects. The implementation specialist from EnvisionWare agrees, although sheepishly admits that it is uncommon for a library to have such a prepared and involved project team. Out of mutual respect for the value of time on both ends, ICPL's project manager has set the stage for optimizing the planning time available.

The implementation specialist reviews the overall project plan, with a proposed target installation date in six or seven weeks. The library's project manager agrees to check ICPL's calendar and respond to the implementation specialist as soon as possible regarding good days to schedule the installation. This schedule will be critical, as the library will need to restrict the public from using the library's computers for a couple of days during the installation itself. The target timeline is also dependent on a timely planning process, but it is based on other successful projects that EnvisionWare has completed with similar libraries.

In addition, the implementation specialist from EnvisionWare notes that he will be emailing an implementation packet to ICPL's project manager outlining the entire process as summarized during the call. It also includes a section of information to be filled out by the library staff, but the EnvisionWare implementation specialist tells the team not to worry—he will go through the packet with them step-by-step to explain it in detail in future calls. ICPL's project manager mentions that the project team has questions, but these questions are mostly functional in nature, regarding how components of the system will work in the library. Given that this first call is more introductory, the implementation specialist requests that those questions be held for the next call but assures the team members that they will have time to address any questions throughout the process. In addition, he notes that if the library has the hardware to set up a test environment, the project team will be able to see exactly how the system will actually work in their library environment.

The team has some silent concerns, as there are still more unknowns than known answers at this point, but all patiently agree to hold their questions until the next call. ICPL's IT staff requests additional information about the requirements for a test environment, and the implementation specialist agrees to send that along with the implementation packet later that day. The next call is scheduled, and the team says their goodbyes.

## Summarize and Highlight Action Items

Once the EnvisionWare staff is off the phone, the project team spends a few more minutes discussing what it has learned thus far:

- The library staff needs to confirm dates for installation. They have previously discussed this and determined that it would be best to have the public computers out of commission from a Tuesday through Thursday to allow the computers to be available for the busy weekends and so that more regular (nonweekend) staff would be available during the installation to work out any issues that arise. The project manager puts forth two possible weeks within the timeframe that EnvisionWare suggested, and the team agrees to verify which is better via email by the next day.

- The project manager confirms that she will forward the implementation packet as soon as she has received it from EnvisionWare but reminds team members that many of the details will be worked out in future calls.

- The project manager confirms the date and time of the next call with the team, noting that the entire team may wish to attend, depending on their schedules and on the detailed agenda yet to be received from EnvisionWare.

As promised, about an hour after the call, the EnvisionWare implementation specialist emails the project manager the promised information:

- A summary of the call

- The implementation packet

- The requirements for a test environment

- The date and time of the next call

And as she had promised, our project manager forwards the information to the rest of the team. Team members (with one exception) have remembered to check their calendars for an installation date and come to a consensus on the best week. Once the dates are confirmed by the final team member, they are forwarded to the library director for final approval for restricting public access to the public computers for those dates. He also approves the installation dates. So the project manager responds to the EnvisionWare implementation specialist with the intended installation dates and a note of enthusiasm for the next call. Through brief email messages, our project manager is able to keep everyone in the loop and aware of what is coming next.

Our project team has two more full-team calls with the implementation specialist, during which their specific questions are answered in more detail. ICPL's project manager and IT staff then have four additional calls with the implementation specialist to work through technical details. The group completes the implementation packet together. The IT staff works with technical support at EnvisionWare to set up the test environment, and the team members are able to see how various library policies could be implemented. Although it is scaled down from their full installation, this test is as close as they will get to actually seeing the product live in their own library prior to implementation. This test enables the team to have some hands-on experience with the system, so members do not have to rely solely on word of mouth to know that it will work for them. Sometimes people do need to see it in order to believe it.

## Common Techniques to Keep in Mind

Without getting lost in the details of this particular project, the project manager wants to point out a few common techniques that can lead to a successful project:

1. Include the team members in all critical pieces of the project without overwhelming them in technical details that they may not understand.

2. Use email to keep the team informed about all communication with the vendor and to share any documents about the project as it moves along.

3. Continue face-to-face meetings on a regular basis to invite questions and to explain the answers fully, so that there are no misunderstandings, as can happen when email is the only form of communication.

4. Emphasize important information and dates through repetition. Even the best of us lose track of details when too many things are happening. Put dates on calendars and use various forms of communication to keep relevant information current in the minds of your team members and minimize surprises.

5. And finally, remember that patience truly is a virtue. With anything new, everyone learns at his or her own pace. As the details unfold, you may need to repeat information or find various ways to communicate with different staff members. In particular, when you are explaining a

technical process to someone who does not adapt easily to new technology, you will need to be patient. Utilize the help of colleagues to get the information across to all staff members in a way that they can understand.

# Chapter 6

# Step Through the Implementation

At this point, you have completed as much of the planning and preparation as you can. The implementation plan is documented, and it seems that both the library team and the vendor are on the same page. All the ordered hardware and software has arrived. And the implementation start date is upon us.

The actual implementation is the most exciting and often the most stressful part of the project. This is the time when it becomes crystal clear whether the solution is going to work as it appeared to during the demo in the exhibit hall, in the video clip on the vendor's website, or even in the small test setting at your library (if you were able to setup a test period). But in your library's full environment, on your computer network, and interacting with all the other systems in your library, how well does it work? Most definitely, there will be problems, unexpected hiccups, and unanticipated conflicts. However, keeping it to one step at a time, steady and patient, you will be able to handle it.

If your project involves having your vendor be on-site to install the new system, then implementation begins the day your vendor arrives at your library. Some projects are implemented remotely by a vendor, using a remote connection to the library's network. In those cases, the actual implementation is often kicked off with a phone call and handled jointly by the vendor and the library staff. Some projects are purchased by the library and installed internally by library staff. No matter how the implementation is done, it begins when software is installed and configured, when hardware is connected, and when network changes pull the new system into the library's environment.

At the appointed date and time, remind your users (staff and the public) that the installation is about to begin. If any resources will be unavailable during the installation, as considered in Chapter 5, one final reminder would be helpful to your users. If new furniture, cables, or other accessories will be used during the implementation, gather all those pieces together so they are at the ready when they are needed.

When all is ready, it is on to step one. Most technology projects have a documented installation process. Either library staff or vendors will begin on page one with step one and work from there.

## Some General Guidelines

Generally, new hardware needs to be physically set up prior to installing the new software. Software needs to be installed on a server or management computer prior to installing software on clients or individual user computers. Here are some best practice guidelines for installing a new system of any type:

- As you work through the installation and configuration, document what you do along the way. Even if you have to make changes down the road due to problems you discover as you implement, it is much easier to note configurations as you go rather than relying on your memory to recreate it all after the fact.

- If a vendor is doing the installation for you, take time to watch what they do to the extent that it is possible. Vendors will likely provide you with documentation at the end of the project, but watching along the way and working with your vendor will teach you a great deal about how the system works.

- If the new system will be installed on multiple user computers, set up just one first and test it before setting up additional computers. This enables you to work out any issues with just one client so the rest of the setup goes more smoothly.

Step through the process one item at a time. Be patient. Communicate openly with your vendor. Identify what you can do to help, and be respectful and flexible as your vendor works to resolve any issues. When in doubt, follow the golden rule: Treat others as you would like to be treated. If stress rises, problems appear, or you find yourself frustrated with how the project is going, keep your emotions in check and focus on one step at a time. Undoubtedly, if you have followed the process in this book so far, your vendor and project team are doing their best to reach your common goal. Treat them as you would like to be treated, invoke some humor if possible, and take it as it comes. Perhaps the best way to explore the initial implementation is to check back with our example team.

# Checking In With Info City Public Library

After working through the planning and configuration documents, the project team is finally welcoming the EnvisionWare implementation specialist to the library. Members are excited to see their planning pay off and eager to see the system take shape in their library.

After introductions are made, the project manager takes the implementation specialist on a brief library tour to show him how the computer network is set up and where the public computers and printers are located. This brings everyone to the same starting point and allows the expectations about the intended outcome to be reiterated. The tour is followed by a team meeting to outline the implementation schedule and get started.

## Installation of Computer Management

Our project manager has asked if she and her IT staff could watch throughout the installation process, so they could learn the details of the system, and that was not a problem at all. The first step is to install the management software on the server. The management software is the central tool that keeps all the rules for the clients and allows the system to keep all the clients in sync. Using the configuration documentation as a guide, the implementation specialist works through the settings on the management console. He sets up the specifications for the various PC areas, the session profiles for library cardholders, the rules for managing guests (users without library cards), and the connection with the integrated library system to check patron records. As the settings are configured, our project manager is able to confirm that they are correct and that no changes have been made to the intended design.

Once the management console is set up for computer clients, the implementation specialist installs the PC reservation software on one public user computer. He configures it to communicate with the management console to pull down the necessary settings. He tests the login functionality and finds that communication with the management console seems to be working.

Next, the implementation specialist installs some limited management software on a staff computer. This software is intended to allow the staff at the reference desk to assist with any questions or basic problems with the system. It is with this step that the technicians encounter their first challenge. At ICPL, the staff computers and the public computers are on physically separate networks. The staff network can communicate with the public network, but not the other way around, for security reasons. Therefore, at this point some firewall rules need to be set to allow the proper communication flow for the staff computers to be able to pull data from this new system on a server on the public network. Fortunately, this problem is not uncommon, and the implementation specialist was able to provide the ports that had to be opened for the communication to occur. One minor hurdle was overcome. One last piece in configuring the staff computer is to add a receipt printer for printing guest passes. As often happens with receipt printers, getting the correct driver installed to print the guest pass properly proves to be a little tricky. But a test guest pass is finally printed, which allows for logins from the public computer. So far, so good.

One more piece of software needs to be installed in order for the public users to create a computer reservation if all the computers are in use by other customers. This software is installed on another computer on the public network, so the network communication is not an issue. A test reservation is made and shows up in the system properly. Here again, a receipt printer is added to allow customers to print their reservation receipts. Since the driver problems were worked out with the previous receipt printer, this one works perfectly the first time. The reservation is tested and functions as expected.

At this point, one major piece of the system (computer management) is in place and has been tested. The settings are documented, and the system appears to be ready to roll out to the rest of the library when the time comes. But so far, the IT staff has only worked with one client computer. They want to ensure that adding a few more clients will not break the system. So they install the client software on two computers in a different area of the library. It does not work perfectly upon first testing, but the IT staff is reminded of a few details as they work out the glitches and note these on their documentation. Things are going fairly well with the PC management implementation.

## Installation of Print Management

The next piece of the system is the print management functionality. Much as with the computer management installation, the print management must first be installed and configured on the server. ICPL's project manager and IT staff shadow the implementation specialist as he installs the software on the server. The network printers need to be added to the server as well and then configured within the print management system.

When all looks correct on the management side, the implementation specialist goes back to one of the test public computers that has the computer management software installed and adds the print management software. Once the client software is in place, he tests it to see if it will successfully intercept a print job and affiliate it with the user signed on to the public computer. It works! So it's on to the next step.

Now, picture this: ICPL has public computers in groups around the library. In addition, the library has two printers to support all of those public computers. Next to each printer in the public area is a print release computer, which library customers will use to find their print job, pay for it, and send it to the printer. Each print release computer needs to have software installed and configured for this new print management system. The configuration on the first print release computer has to be adjusted a couple of times before it properly communicates with the print management software and the master print queue. But before long, that too is working. A test print job is sent from the client computer, picked up by the print management software and held in the queue, and then released after the user logs in at the print release station. Yay!

ICPL charges customers to print. To facilitate payment, they want to accept either cash, through a coin and bill acceptor, or money debited from a customer's print account. The library has purchased two new coin and bill acceptors with the EnvisionWare system, one for each print release station. The next step is to configure the coin and bill acceptor so the system will require payment before releasing the print job. The implementation specialist from EnvisionWare connects the hardware and sets it up to communicate with the print release station, then configures the system to count the pages and calculate payment based on the library's cost policies. Another test print job is sent to the print release station, and the implementation specialist elects to pay via cash. Coins are added to the coin and bill acceptor to meet the required total, and the job is released to the printer. The basic functionality seems to be in place.

## Installation of Print Accounting

In addition to allowing payment with cash at the coin and bill acceptor, ICPL wants to allow customers to deposit money into a

print account and then pay for printouts by deducting money from this account. The library also wants to give each customer 50 cents worth of free printing every day. EnvisionWare has a system for these functions called the accounting and authentication module (AAM). The module is first installed on the server as a central database and then set up to allow for both deposit and automatic daily allocation.

In addition, the print release stations are modified to communicate with the AAM database. A test patron account is created in the AAM database, and a test print job is sent from that patron account. At the print release station, the system is able to pull up the balance on the patron's account and provide additional options for payment. Communication has been established, and money is successfully deducted from the account to pay for the print job. The implementation is looking good!

There are still two more pieces to add. First, the print release station has to be modified yet again to offer library customers the option of using the coin and bill acceptor to add money to their print accounts. Once that option is in place, some additional functionality is added to the management software at the staff reference desks so staff can access the customers' AAM accounts. Staff may need to assist with checking accounts and/or adding money to an account if problems arise. However, as with the previous staff computer configurations, IT staff need to make some changes to the network so that the staff computers can communicate with the AAM database on the public server. Luckily, it is once again a straightforward matter of opening up some ports to provide the necessary access.

## Extended Testing

When it seems all the main components are in place, the library staff on the project team assist with some more extensive testing before rolling out the system to the rest of the public computers. A couple of computers in each PC area are added, and the necessary area-specific rules are put in place and tested. These include age-restricted access as well as ILS-based restrictions on patron accounts in suboptimal standing (due to fines owed or other concerns that affect the patron's access to library services), in accordance with library policy. Printing in both black and white and color must be tested to ensure the proper payment amounts are charged. Staff also test to make sure that sessions can be extended when no one else is waiting but not when someone has a reservation. Library staff members are critical to assisting with accurate testing, as they can ensure that their public computing needs are being met by the system.

Our project manager is happy to see the implementation progressing fairly well so far. She knows that she needs to stay on top of the project so that the implementation will continue to be successful as it moves along.

# Chapter 7

# Plan Again

Step by step, the implementation is underway. In Chapter 5, you created your implementation plan. Whether it was created through guidelines from your vendor or your own project management resources, you have some documentation that outlines how your project will be implemented. Do you have that documentation handy? (If not, find it and pull it out.)

In order for your project to be successful, it is important to follow through on your plan. In the planning stages, you considered a variety of details that are important to your project. You made decisions about how the project should be configured. You noted how various library policies should be implemented within the project. How are you doing with the actual implementation as you compare it to your original plan? Take a look at the intended timeline from your implementation plan—how does it look? Is the implementation taking longer than you expected due to unanticipated challenges? Almost every technology system implementation is going to encounter some challenges. With proper planning, most of these will be minor issues that can be addressed quickly so the project stays on task. But some problems may arise that require more significant changes to your plan. So it is all the more important to take a step back in the middle of your implementation and analyze your progress.

## Check Your Pulse

For a number of years, I was a member of a fitness center called Curves, and I worked out there a few times each week. (Well, OK, I didn't make it every week, but I tried!) The workout is a circuit of resistance weight machines. You start anywhere on the circuit and listen to the audio cues. You will spend 30 seconds on a machine, and then you will be told to move to the next station. In between the weight machines, you find a cardio-pad where you jog in place or do any sort of cardio exercise to keep your heart rate steady. Every 10 or 15 minutes, an audio cue will talk you through checking your pulse. You then compare your pulse rate to a poster on the wall to determine whether you are working out too hard, too lightly, or just right. If you are working out too hard and your pulse rate is too high, you should slow down your workout. If you are working out too lightly and your pulse rate is too low, you should push yourself harder. If you are working out just right and your pulse rate is in the correct range, keep up the good work.

Believe it or not, implementing a technology solution also creates a kind of pulse. It is very important to take a moment in the middle of the project and check the pulse of the project. Is it moving too fast and are too many details being overlooked? If so, slow it down. Is it moving too slowly and falling way behind on the intended timeline? If so, try to increase the rate of productivity. Or is it moving along just right, and things are under control? If so, keep up the good work!

# Library Responsibilities

One reason technology projects take longer than originally planned is that during implementation, it often becomes clear that the library needs to make some changes to its infrastructure for the system to function properly. Perhaps the library met the lower end of the technical requirements for the new system and was hoping that would be enough. Then during implementation, the IT staff found that although the system would run on their machines, it was unacceptably slow. In this case, the library may need to upgrade its hardware in order for the system to run better.

# Vendor Responsibilities

Alternately, sometimes the vendor discovers problems during the implementation that keep the system from functioning the way that it should. Resolving the problems takes time and slows down the overall progress. This can happen when a vendor rolls out a new product to a customer for the first time or with a specific set of parameters for the first time. For example, many library vendors integrate their systems with many different integrated library systems (ILS). A system may complete the basic testing to be compliant with the different ILS vendors, but the first actual implementation in a library with a specific ILS might uncover unexpected problems. In this case, the vendor would need to do some additional development work to make its system work for the library. Depending on the vendor, the system, and the development needed, this may delay the timeline extensively. As I have learned from so many different experiences, it is just another situation where planning ahead, asking questions before implementation, and even using a test environment (when possible) can help work through all types of challenges.

# Plan Again and Move On

Further still, some systems require the coordination of multiple systems in order to get everything set up the way it should be. The library may need to make some changes, the vendor may need to get some fixes in place, and perhaps a third party will need to assist with some configuration changes. Most importantly, be sure to update your documentation to reflect any and all changes made. Your documentation must be an accurate reflection of your project implementation. You will depend on this documentation in the future, so keep it current and accurate.

If even the best laid plans do not lead to a smooth implementation, remain calm and reasonable throughout the troubleshooting process. Assigning blame certainly will not help. The best thing you can do is be flexible and communicate openly. The original plan will undoubtedly have to be adjusted. In order to achieve success, work together with your vendor and staff to find the best possible compromise. When working through a difficult challenge mid-implementation, it is very easy for emotions and frustration to impede progress. If you've chosen a vendor with whom you have a good relationship, it will go a long way toward reaching a resolution.

## Spotlight: Vendor Relationships

As an IT manager in a library, I am always careful to select vendors with whom I feel comfortable. The importance of that relationship has always been clear to me, and it was highlighted once again when I was working with a vendor that was fairly new to me. I purchased the time- and print-management system from EnvisionWare for the public library where I work. I planned the project vigilantly, and the implementation was actually quite smooth. We had a few post-implementation issues to work through, but overall, the library was up and running quickly with the new system.

A couple weeks later, I was away from the library, attending the Computers in Libraries conference. Shortly after I arrived at my hotel, I started receiving urgent phone calls from the library about the system: The system was down, would come back up for a bit, and go back down again—what was going on? I tried some remote troubleshooting but was not getting very far. When the exhibit hall opened at the conference, I made a beeline for the EnvisionWare booth. I spoke to the first person I met and tried to explain our problems. She told me I should speak with her colleague, who was busy with another customer at the moment. I waited (as patiently as I could) until I was able to introduce myself to her colleague, who had the most technical expertise of anyone at the booth. And sure enough, he was very knowledgeable about the system and concerned about my problems. It took some time, but eventually we were able to identify the source of the problems at my library. He made some phone calls and even handed off his cell phone to me so I could speak directly with his colleagues who could help.

I feel strongly that the additional connections I made with EnvisionWare staff during that time elevated my regard for its systems. Any system can have problems, but a vendor's willingness to spend whatever time it takes to resolve those issues speaks loudly to me as a customer. And truth be told, we have had almost no concerns with the system since then.

What does your project pulse look like? If you need to make adjustments to the plan, be flexible and realistic. Minor (or major) changes now will surely benefit the project as a whole in the end. Most often, mid-project alterations are fairly minor. They may delay things only by a day or two and often not even that much. But if you do not know where you are, you will find it more difficult to stay on track.

# Checking In With Info City Public Library

The team is now mid-implementation, and the project manager wants to ensure that the project continues on track and that any outstanding issues are addressed. The major components are configured and undergoing testing. The process certainly has not been without problems and challenges, but most have been manageable.

The library staff members still have to complete the implementation on the rest of the library's public computers. Their testing has not brought forth any major issues that need attention. So the project manager meets with the project team to check the pulse of the project.

## Take Stock of the Project Status

Together, the project team creates a list of questions to ask, issues to resolve, and other items to do before rolling out the system library-wide. Although it seems that, for the most part, the implementation is moving along smoothly, there are still some questions and some things that need attention. At this point, our team's list includes the following:

- Customize the login screens for computer management.

- Add the library's Internet Policy to the public website so it is accessible by the computer management software, which will direct customers to read and accept the policy before providing access.

- Make the auto-created guest pass PIN more obvious after a guest logs in (it gets lost on the screen easily, so many guest pass users do not write it down for use at the print release station).

- Export ILS patron list to be imported into the accounting and authentication module (AAM).

- Get the copier technician to help with coin and bill acceptors and bar code readers for copy machines.

- Add bar code scanner to print release stations.

After creating their list of outstanding questions, the project team looks back over its project plan. Nothing appears to be completely out of line. The project could certainly continue along its plan and likely hit the intended "go live" date, depending on how the implementation specialist handles some of their questions. In order to find out, they meet with him to share their list and find out what else they might be missing. He is receptive to their questions and assures them that all these issues can be handled in a timely fashion. He also shares what is left to do on his end:

- Install and configure reports.

- Set up bar code scanners on copy machines to allow payment from AAM account for copies.

- Investigate wireless printing setup.

- Train staff.

- Plan to "go live" with the public.

At this point, both the team and the vendor feel reasonably satisfied with how the project implementation is going. There is still a great deal of work to do, but they still have time with their vendor on-site. So the project plan is continuing as intended.

# Chapter 8

# Customize and Finalize the System

Once you have taken the pulse of your project, you can determine what your next steps must be. Just as during a workout, a high pulse rate requires you to slow down and a low pulse rate requires you to step it up. During the time it takes to analyze how things are going, you should outline for yourself what needs to be done to continue along the project path to completion, get the project back on track, or modify the project based on unanticipated circumstances. I have an example project to help illustrate each of these scenarios. These projects were all completed at libraries with which I am familiar.

## Implementation on Schedule

During some projects, everything moves along as it should and the pulse of the project is right on target. Perhaps some minor adjustments need to be made to the project plan. Or a few things need to be added to a to-do list of unresolved items so they are addressed. When projects are going well, this is the stage for the finishing touches—those extra little tweaks to make things just a bit easier or just a bit nicer for your customers. You can customize the look-and-feel of the new system to better reflect your library's character. You can add some labels or signs to help your customers get accustomed to the new system. Even providing something special for the staff (such as sweet treats) to acknowledge that the work is going well helps keep things moving along smoothly.

## Example: Self-Check Installation

One library found that it was increasingly busy at the circulation desk but also had limited space and funds. It wanted to explore a self-check machine but would only have room for one. The library had electromagnetic security so it would not need to worry about radio frequency identification (RFID) at the time, but an option to upgrade in the future was welcome. All options were carefully examined, and a vendor was chosen for one self-check unit.

The project leader carefully planned for the implementation, documenting as she went along and communicating with staff. She was frequently in touch with the vendor to ensure all the details were clear and questions answered. When her project team had questions or suggestions, these were considered and discussed, and the entire group was involved in the decisions.

The system was ordered—both hardware and software. When the hardware arrived and the vendor came on-site to do the installation, all went extremely smoothly. The system was installed and configured according to the specifications determined in the planning stages. Before the system was made available for the public, the vendor did some hands-on training for the project team (and other staff). Staff members had a chance to try out the various features of the system that their customers would be using and ensure that all was working.

When everyone was satisfied, the system was put into operation in the public area. To add some appeal to the new system, library staff members brought colorful helium balloons to draw attention to the area. Customers were invited and encouraged to try it out as they neared the checkout area at the library. Many customers who were among the first to use the system had a successful experience, and the future looked bright for self-checkout at this library.

This particular project went very well for the library. By the time it was installed, the staff had any questions answered and had some idea of what to expect. They worked to promote the system to the customers to encourage its use. When the mid-project pulse check showed that things were on track for completion, some little extras were added, such as staff being assigned to assist with the new system. Library staff ensured there was a small table near the new machine for customers to place their items during the check-out process. The vendor even commented that this particular installation was one of his smoothest ever, due mostly to the pre-paredness and attentiveness of the project leader.

The project was not without resistance or concerns; the public had to be trained in the use of the system, and some adapted better than others. The workflow of the circulation staff members changed with the addition of the unit. The security system in the library came into question and was even disabled with the addition of the unit, due to the desires of the library. Everything that is new comes with challenges and adjustments. However, this particular project was completed quite smoothly, and much of the success was attributed to good planning, attention to detail, and communication.

# Implementation Detoured

Many technology projects encounter a situation where the project implementation takes a bit of a detour along the way. During the mid-project pulse check, you discover that you have fallen behind schedule due to additional work that has to be done by the library, by the vendor, or some combination of the two. This could be an instance where the library has to complete some hardware upgrades or network reconfigurations before the system functions properly. Perhaps when the hardware for the new system is unpacked and set up, you discover that something was damaged in transit, so that a replacement needs to be ordered.

## Example: Server Virtualization

Every organization relies heavily on its technology infrastructure to do its work. In a library, everyone notices if the website goes down, if staff loses access to the integrated library systems (ILS), or if customers cannot search the online catalog. The computer servers that manage these critical resources are vital to the library staff's ability to provide service.

The IT staff at one library found its server environment becoming difficult to manage. The servers were about four years old, and some of them were beginning to suffer from hardware failure. In addition, the library director was looking to cut spending and conserve energy as much as possible. Therefore, this library decided to investigate virtualization. A virtual environment would enable the library to convert many of its physical servers to virtual servers, which run on much less physical hardware and consume less energy. In addition, the library would be able to move its data to a storage area network, condensing its data storage to an efficient device.

After researching the options, the library decided to purchase VMware as the software to manage its virtual environment. Two new physical servers were purchased to host VMware and a storage area network (SAN) for the combined data storage. This solution would provide the library with flexibility into the future. The library ordered the recommended equipment (software, servers, and SAN) from the chosen vendor, and the project was scheduled and moved into the implementation phase.

As the project team began working with the vendor's implementation engineer during the planning phase, the engineer advised that even though the originally quoted equipment would work, there were better ways to optimally support their network needs. Therefore, the engineer recommended a slight change to the design of the SAN. This modification slightly increased the overall project cost, but the library's project manager agreed to the revised proposal, as it would save the library money in the end by providing them with a solution that was a better fit.

However, this change delayed the project by a few weeks. The SAN hardware had to be reordered to meet the new specifications, and therefore the delivery of the SAN was pushed back. In addition, the engineer was occupied with other projects on his schedule, so he would not be available to implement the project for a couple of weeks after the new SAN hardware arrived at the library. The slightly higher cost, the delay in the arrival of the hardware due to the reordering, and the delay in the schedule for the implementation caused a minor detour from the original project plan. However, with a little flexibility and patience, all of the pieces fell into place, and the end result has proven to be a success.

# Implementation Derailed

Some technology projects come to an unexpected halt somewhere during the implementation process, due to circumstances that cannot be reconciled in a timely fashion. Whether the issues fall with the library, the vendor, or both, some issues have a big enough impact that the only option is to stop the implementation and explore the problems in further detail before continuing.

## Example: Cash Management System Installation

One library discovered that it did not have adequate accountability for the money that was collected at the circulation desk. Staff would collect money from customers to pay library fines and fees, mark the patron account paid in the ILS, and then put the cash or check in the cash register, which had no correlation back to why the money was collected or by whom. The ILS and the cash register were essentially separate entities, with no connection between them. The cash register drawers were reconciled daily but not compared to the ILS reports of money collected. To address this problem, the library purchased a cash management system.

The cash management system supports the session initiation protocol (SIP) to communicate between the ILS and the cash software system. It can look up fines and fees owed by patron bar code, report back to the ILS when a payment has been collected from a patron, and keep records of the payment details in its own database.

When the library worked through the planning for the project, the project manager decided to opt for remote installation in order to save some money. She was comfortable with the technology in the library and felt confident she could handle the on-site configuration. The library also had an extra computer in the staff workroom that could be set up as a test computer, which would allow the IT staff to get the system configured properly and give staff time to become comfortable with it.

Library staff had conference calls with the vendor to go through some initial planning. The vendor sent an implementation document, which the library staff filled out to assist with the process. Even though IT staff members were comfortable with the technology in the library, they quickly learned how little they understood about a point-of-sale system. Generally, libraries do not sell merchandise. Library staff collect fines and fees as needed, but there is not much to be sold. Therefore, the IT staff had to learn the language of cash management. Cash management systems maintain an inventory of items sold, such as a library bag. But in libraries, paying fines and fees must also be an option in the inventory, as it is another situation when the library collects money.

The cash management system had to be set up for handling cash, checks, and credit cards. It had to communicate not only with the ILS (which was one of the easier parts) but also with some additional software to connect with a merchant account for processing credit card payments, and that configuration was another challenge. The project team had numerous questions, and many things to learn in order to understand this new system. To compound the problem, the implementation specialist from the vendor did not fit well with the library staff. Communication seemed difficult and expectations were unclear.

Nonetheless, the library persevered through the initial installation working with the vendor remotely. Concerns became apparent early on in the implementation process. The biggest problem appeared when the system did not integrate as fully with the ILS as the library thought it would from day one. Library staff learned that its ILS did not provide itemized fine information to the cash management software, and this was a deal-breaker for the library. The library needed to allow customers to pay specific fines (or portions thereof) and needed the system to report back to the ILS patron record which individual items were paid. This functionality was available with other ILSs, so why wasn't it possible for this library?

Consequently, midway through the implementation process, the installation was halted to consult with the development teams for both the ILS vendor and the cash management vendor. Discussions ensued for weeks, which stretched into months. Both development teams created new software, and the resulting system was tested. Various versions from both vendors were made available, and the products were eventually tweaked to provide the functionality that the library had expected at the beginning of the process.

It was at least six months after the product was purchased by the library before the necessary functionality was available to handle the itemized fines, and it was almost a year later that the system was finally implemented in the library. While the lack of itemized fines was the biggest problem, there were other smaller problems as well. Not all the features that the library wanted were available when the system went live, as some were left for future development efforts.

What is the lesson from this experience? There are a few:

1. This is a prime example where the system did not meet the library expectations, although this was not initially obvious to either party. The cash management vendor knew that the itemized fines feature worked with other ILSs. And the library was not familiar enough with cash management software to even know to ask for specific details on that issue in the first place. The library could have benefited by doing more research prior to purchasing the system.

2. Whether the problem was primarily a personality clash, a perceived lack of knowledge on the part of the implementation specialist, or too many unspoken expectations, this library did end up requesting to work with a different staff member at the vendor company in order to keep the implementation process moving forward.

3. This situation clearly demonstrates the value of a test environment setup, in which a problem such as this could be discovered and further troubleshooting could be accomplished without disrupting the library's daily business.

4. It was also very helpful in this situation that the library was a current customer of the vendor for the cash management system. Contacts and relationships with staff at the vendor company enabled progress to occur. Having a vendor actually make time to fit in new development for your library is the exception, and that is part of the reason the timeline was extended as far as it was. Give and take was required from both the library and the vendor in this situation. Patience enabled the library to get a better product in the end.

The library does not consider this a failed project; the cash management system is now installed and being used after all. However, it was a much-delayed project due to many circumstances. On the positive side, the library discovered it was the first customer for the ILS to use that particular cash management system, so the work will enable other libraries with the same ILS to better manage their cash flow.

# The Last Lap

As you are working through the finishing touches, remember to work through the entire system. Install the project on all the computers where it needs to be. Tweak those last few changes on all of the clients. Test out each instance of the system. If you try to cut corners in the final stages, no doubt your customers will find the pieces you missed. Wouldn't it better for you to take the extra time to go through all that so you know before they do? You may still miss something along the way, and the true testing will be up to your customers. But pay attention to the details. They do matter.

## Spotlight: Finding Others People's Mistakes

When working with a vendor, there is nothing I dislike more than finding a mistake in a document the vendor has given me. Honest mistakes will happen, but careless ones should not. I recently received a price quote for a new system from a vendor, and I found that there were items missing. The quote included both hardware and software, and the specific configuration of the hardware was critical to the project's success. When vendors are putting together the quote for a system, why should I be the one to specify every single detail? They are the experts. If I choose to accept the quote and purchase the system, I will be paying them for the hardware, software, and personnel to install and configure it. Yet when I am the one telling the vendor which items need to be included (based on previous conversations with the firm and/or my own research), I am left wondering who has more expertise.

At the end of the final lap, there may be items left undone. There might be follow-up tasks that will not affect the live system but still need to be completed or questions that need to be answered. Document these items carefully. Make sure you and your vendor know what the outstanding items are and who is responsible for handling them. Depending on the vendor, post-implementation follow-up may be left to another team within the company, such as the support team. Having your items documented enables you to take an active role in pursuing the completion of these remaining tasks after the implementation specialist leaves your site.

# Checking In With Info City Public Library

Our project team is finishing up its mid-project pulse check after doing some more extensive testing of the system in place. Members have a list of seven items that need to be addressed, none of which seem complicated enough to derail or even detour their project plan.

The first order of business is to follow the client installation procedures and get the system installed and configured on the rest of the public computers in the library. The IT staff set about on this task, having assisted on the previous test implementations along the way.

Meanwhile, the project manager works with the implementation specialist to discuss and work through the list of remaining items. Customizing the login screens and pointing the system to the library's Internet Policy are both accomplished via straightforward configurations on the management console. However, the ability to customize the guest pass PIN login screen is not currently available; that option is added to the enhancement request list.

The library's copier vendor arrives to connect the new bar code scanners to the copy machines. The scanners are actually network devices that communicate with the database where the print account funds for customers are stored. The connection proves to be a new challenge for the copier vendor, but he will not be defeated. Once the bar code scanners are connected, the implementation specialist configures them for use by the AAM accounts in the system.

As the client installations are completed, the project team members are recruited to work through the additional testing. The

IT staff adds bar code scanners to the print release and reservation stations to make logins easier.

Discussion ensues about the export of patron records from the ILS so the accounts would exist in the AAM database for printing. Without an export/import of patrons, each patron would have to initiate his own account before he could deposit funds or receive the daily free printing allocation. In the future, this will be done automatically as new patrons are added, but for patrons already in the system, the project team wants to make the process as simple as possible. As the team members explore the issue with their implementation specialist, the project manager learns that the records required for the print database are quite minimal. Therefore, she is able to work with the export tools for her ILS to get the records she needs to populate the AAM database.

As the system is being finalized, testing again finds a few problems, but these are limited to some individual details at specific computers—those repeated installations can miss some details when attempted speed gives way to carelessness. At least these problems are uncovered through team testing and are easily corrected before the public starts using the system.

A couple of tasks remain, but none is critical to the public's ability to use the new system. In order to stay on track, it is time to shift gears and move on to training and preparation for going live.

# Chapter 9

# Train Staff, Prepare Users, and Promote

Remember that you did not learn how to use the new system overnight, and neither will the rest of your staff nor your customers. Who will need to learn the new system? Will it be used primarily by the staff or the customers? Will the staff need to assist the customers in using it? Even if the system is mostly self-explanatory, it will be important to provide information to your customers about it as well.

## Staff Training

Once the new system is in place, take some time to train your staff members on how it works before expecting them to use it. A common complaint among staff members in any institution is that they are not provided with enough training on the technology they are expected to use. Just as it took you and your project team a great deal of time to research systems and become familiar with the chosen system, the rest of the staff also needs to become familiar with it. The staff will not likely need to know every technical detail involved, but all staff should get some awareness training. In addition, staff members using the system in any way—whether directly or assisting customers—should get some in-depth training on what they will need to know.

One of the better ways to do this is to set aside time and prepare an actual training schedule. If some staff members require more advanced training than others, you can set up a couple of different training agendas to meet different needs. Ideally, provide hands-on training to take staff through the new system step-by-step and show them how it works. In addition, provide time for questions, as your staff will undoubtedly have some.

Often when you hire a vendor to install a new system, the vendor will include time for staff training as part of the installation. Having the vendor train your staff directly is priceless. The vendors is the expert on the system and will be the best resource to answer questions about it. However, one important note is that the project manager should be present for the training classes as well. Even though it seems like this could be a golden opportunity for the project manager to handle other tasks, she is the one who knows how the system will be implemented at your library. All the details regarding policies and procedures are determined locally. Your vendor has implemented what he was told, but your staff might very well have questions about how the local implementation affects library policies and procedures, and the project manager will be a key resource in providing the correct information from the start. So have the vendor provide the expertise about the system directly to the staff but have the project manager there to fill in the how's and why's regarding local implementation.

# Ongoing Training and Tips for Staff

It is important to remember that staff training is not a one-time event. The initial training will provide the information needed to get started. However, once staff members start using the system on a regular basis, they will have more questions. If it is a system that your customers will be using, new scenarios will be discovered that were not covered in training.

Therefore, consider creating a way for sharing ongoing tips— perhaps on a staff intranet, via email, or through follow-up "learning lunches" for in-person questions and answers. At my library, we try to use all three venues for sharing information. We have a web-based staff intranet to which staff can post information. The value in this web-based tool is that it is searchable and archived for a long period of time. However, not all staff members are in the habit of checking the intranet on a regular basis, so important and timely information is still sometimes sent out via email. In addition, we try to schedule "learning lunches" from time to time. These are meetings that we offer at lunch time for staff to attend, bring their lunch, and have some extra training on a system or resource at the library. They provide a unique learning experience for those who are willing to give up their lunch hour to get detailed information on a topic of interest.

# Customer Training

If the new system is one that your customers will use, then you will need to share information about it with them as well. Hopefully by this point, you have already done some promotion of the new system to your customers. Did you have to close the library at all in order to install the new system? Or were some resources (public computers or the online catalog) unavailable during implementation? Then you likely explained to your customers at the time that the resources would be unavailable and why.

If the system is one that customers will have to use regularly, such as a self-checkout machine or a computer reservation system, being present to assist them will be the best approach in the beginning. However, you might also want to have signs and other written instructions available to help them get started on their own. Generally, systems intended for library customers are designed for self-service. But with anything new, many of your customers will require assistance at first, and some for quite a while. Each customer is different and will interpret the system differently. Many will never read the signs you create, and some will go so far as to move them out of the way without reading them— and then have trouble.

Even if the new system is one that will be used solely by the staff, I have found that it is very helpful to make your customers aware that the staff is using something new. Create some signs that say something like "Please be patient with us as we are learning a new system today" and post them at your service desks. This might spark some tolerance from your customers when the staff takes a bit longer than usual to handle a question or transaction.

# Promote the Positive

It is important to tell your customers why you are doing something new. This is true of the staff as well. And the answer is easy, if you've followed the process here: The reason you are putting in a new system is because you discovered the library had a need. You did not just install a new system because it was cool. You did it for a reason, and you should be able to share that reason fairly easily with your customers and staff.

Sometimes the reasons are obvious to the customers, and other times they are not. Explain to them all the benefits that they and the library will gain from the new system. Promote the positive. Undoubtedly, some will discover negatives on their own. They might even focus on these negatives and use them to criticize the library's decision to implement the system. Following a structured process as outlined in this book will give your library the resources it needs to manage the complaints as they arise. And they will.

In addition, some of your staff may not like the new system. It is important that they understand the reasons for the new system and can share them with your customers in a positive way. Having a staff member complain about a new system to your customers will greatly hurt your relationship with your community. So if you have staff members who openly disagree with the library's decision, talk with them about their concerns until you can get them on the same page. Hopefully by including a team of people in the planning and being open with the staff along the way, you will be able to overcome any long-standing opposition.

## Spotlight: Setting the Stage for Success

Often the success or failure of a project, and whether it is accepted or rejected by the staff and customers, can be attributed to upper management in the library. There are two extremes:

A. A director who reprimands failures and allows staff to do only projects that he wants to do and only if they are done his way

B. A director who is open to anyone's ideas and allows his staff to just try anything new, with the understanding that if it doesn't work out, oh well, try again next time

Director A sends the message to his staff that failure is not an option and that he knows what is best for the library. Certainly, Director A may think that he has the library's best interests in mind. However, he may be unaware of the message his attitude sends to his staff, which is that he does not respect or trust them. This approach may invoke fear and cooperation in some staff members, and it may invoke rebellion and frustration in others. Projects implemented in an environment under Director A will often be resented by the staff, and those who are not afraid to do so may openly criticize the new system to customers.

Director B sends the message to his staff that everyone has good ideas, and he is willing to try anything new, risking possible failure. Generally, Director B wants his staff to feel respected and capable. He is willing to try new projects knowing that they might not all be successful, and this approach is often appreciated by staff members. The danger here is that the director may fail to assert authority when decisions are needed, and too much leniency can lead to chaos. Projects implemented in an environment under Director B may not be well-planned or managed unless there is an established structure in place to require accountability.

I believe that the place a few steps above Director B (but well below Director A) is where you find a productive working environment. The director must be willing to try new ideas, allow mistakes, and have open communication with his staff. This will bring out the best in the staff. However, new ideas must also be within reason, well-planned, and implemented within a structure that includes checks and balances, such as the process presented in this book.

It is important to include in your project plan adequate time and resources for training and promotion of the new system. This tells both your staff and your customers that you know this is something new and that you value their involvement in making the project successful. You cannot succeed without them!

# Checking In With Info City Public Library

Our project team is now putting the final touches on the system and testing each computer in the system. Meanwhile, our project manager is putting together the final staff training schedule. She works with the department heads to gather as many staff members as possible for training, prioritizing those who work in the public services areas and who will need to assist customers with signing on to a computer and printing.

Our team is lucky in that there is a computer lab to use for hands-on training for staff. Our project manager puts together three groups of staff training sessions, and the EnvisionWare implementation specialist is on-site to conduct the training. As the implementation itself is nearly complete, this gives the staff time to learn the system and ask questions before the public starts using the system.

The staff training is planned entirely by EnvisionWare, and the content covers all the various pieces of the system. First, staff members learn to use the system as the customers would, both signing on to a computer and printing, as well as paying for print-outs. Then they have an opportunity to see the staff side as well: assisting with reservations, managing the sessions and computers in use, and managing customers' print money accounts.

Our project manager is present during the sessions to hear the questions and answer those that pertain to local policies and decisions, of which there are some. Most have to do with handling guest users and guest passes, and why they are handled differently than library cardholders. As with many libraries implementing a reservation system for the first time, ICPL has never before restricted access to its public computers. Therefore, the project manager carefully explains the policies and how they align with the library's overall mission. ICPL values providing fair access to its computer technology. Any resident (of any age) who lives in the service area can get a library card. Therefore, residents do not have to get a guest pass. Guest passes are intended for true guests in the area, visitors who are not eligible for a library card. As with other ICPL policies, preference is always given to residents of the library's service area, since residents pay the taxes to support the library operations. Therefore, it is not unreasonable to allow library cardholders more time on the computers (a default 60-minute session for library cardholders and a 30-minute session for guests). When there is no one waiting for a computer, a library cardholder can automatically extend his session, whereas a guest will need to request a new guest pass from a staff member.

The open discussions about these policies and why they were set satisfies most staff members. And not too surprisingly, many staff members leave the training session commenting that they like the new system and that it seems quite easy to use. Only time will tell if that holds true after the system goes live.

Meanwhile, other team members are finalizing details on the signs for the public area to help get customers started with the new system. The customers know the system is coming, due to previous promotion about the system. Some do not understand why they will need their library card to get on a computer with the new system, while others are pleased that they will be able to reserve a computer when all are in use. The process will be an adjustment for both customers and staff, but the team is doing everything it can to prepare everyone. As the appointed hour to "go live" approaches, a sense of excitement is building in the library.

# Chapter 10

# Launch the New System

Going live! This is the time everyone has been waiting for, some with excitement, others with fear. All of your planning has been leading up to this moment. The configuration decisions have been made, the implementation details have been completed, and your staff has been trained. The only thing left is to flip the switch and turn on the new system. The need that the library originally identified is about to be fulfilled by this new system. The library (staff, customers, and community) will now benefit from all the new features available with the system.

## A Public Launch

Depending upon the type of system you are implementing, the launch itself will vary. If the new system is one that your customers will interact with directly, then your "go live" may be a very public event. For example, if the system is a new ILS or a new self-check machine, then you will want to celebrate the launch of the new system in a way that includes your customers.

In this situation, you have undoubtedly already done some promotion in anticipation of the new system. You have told your customers that it is coming and likely fielded many questions along the way. You have promoted the new features that will be available with the system. The launch itself is a continuation of that process, expanded to include any customers who missed the earlier promotions.

## Be Present

I have only one rule for public launch days: Be present. This rule always reminds me of a 1994 *Family Circus* cartoon where Dolly explains to her younger brother Jeffy some important wisdom, "Yesterday's the past, tomorrow's the future, but today is a GIFT. That's why it's called the present."[1] I'd like to draw Bill Keane's wisdom out to its application in the workplace. Each day is an opportunity to be present in that day and give all you can to the matter at hand. Being present, especially on a day when there is a greater potential for challenges, speaks volumes about the importance of the new system, your appreciation for the work done on the new system, and your support for ensuring that all goes smoothly.

Certainly the project manager and entire project team should be present, assisting with details as needed. If you have had an on-site installation by your vendor, usually the vendor is present on the day the system goes live as well to handle any problems and answer questions. You should also have upper management present to offer support. Have extra staff members out in the public area where the new system is installed to provide assistance and support—to both the customers and each other—with the new system.

Being present sends the message to your customers that you understand this is something new, and you are going to assist them through the transition. In addition, it sends an important message to your staff that you are not just throwing a new system at them and leaving them to fend for themselves. You are there to support them. You will work with them. And together, you will succeed.

Being present also provides a sense of calm and confidence. You do not need to look over everyone's shoulder to ensure they are doing everything correctly. You are there to offer assistance if needed. Otherwise, you are there to provide assurance to your colleagues, with a simple pat on the back and expression of gratitude for their professionalism.

## The Fear Factor

Does the thought of launching a new system publicly create anxiety in anyone reading this? What if the new system doesn't work and all the customers get angry? Could you handle all the criticism? Do you have a plan B?

Well, if that describes you, hang on just a minute: Did you forget already that you have done extensive testing on the system? Did you fail to give yourself credit for all the planning that you did? Now, if you have disregarded the previous chapters of this book, then you have reason to be anxious! But if you have followed through this planning process, then you have very little to worry about at this point. You have made careful decisions, paid attention to the details, and taken time to test. Aside from some minor issues, your launch should go very smoothly. In fact, with proper planning, this is the easiest day of the whole process.

## Go for It!

The appointed time has come. Turn on the new system and let your customers (and staff) start using it. Observe how the new system is received and how well it works. Provide assistance and answer questions as needed. Make the rounds, if the system is in use in various parts of the library. Listen to people's comments and make mental notes about what works well and what does not. For the most part, you should be pleasantly surprised by how well the launch goes.

Some customers may be right up front, ready to test out the new system and see if it lives up to their expectations. Their expectations may or may not be realistic. Their experience is what counts, not their expectations. They may be very open to the new system, or they may complain every step of the way. On the other hand, there may be some customers who refuse even to try using the new system and insist that staff handle them as they used to. Change is always hard. Offer these customers the hand-holding they need to go through using the new system, and with any luck, they will soon find the confidence to use it themselves.

# A Quiet Launch

If your system is one that mostly affects the staff or does not require as much direct interaction with your customers, perhaps you will choose to do a quiet launch. In this case, you would not necessarily make a big public announcement about your new system. You would certainly alert your staff members and ensure that they are trained and ready. You would still need to be present to assist your staff and answer questions.

This type of a launch might be considered for a new staff intranet, a new telephone system, or a new point-of-sale system. In addition, it could be used for new services such as chat reference or even a new website redesign. Starting quietly gives the staff a chance to get used to the system before being inundated by high-volume use. If the system is one that the staff must use to interact with the customers in person, I recommend posting signs like "Please be patient with us while we learn a new telephone system today" (as suggested in Chapter 9). This lets your customers know that the staff is working hard but trying to learn something new, which might help them be patient if transactions take a little longer than usual.

With a quiet launch, you need to focus on how your staff manages the new system. Observe them and collect their feedback. Be patient with your staff, and do whatever you can to support them in making a positive transition to the new system.

Most importantly, remember that with any new system, you must give it time. On day one, you will hear the most complaints (and hopefully the most compliments as well). As time progresses and everyone becomes more comfortable, the complaints will dissipate. The comments that remain will likely be good and honest feedback about the new system. We will address the ongoing evaluation process further in the next two chapters.

# Checking In With Info City Public Library

Our project team has completed its training and is ready to launch the new computer and print management system. The team is excited and feels that the system has been fairly well-received by the staff during training. The EnvisionWare implementation specialist is still on site and will be around through the "go live" period to help with any issues.

So the big moment arrives, and the staff brings up all the public computers for use by the customers. Most customers are just grateful to have access to the internet again! Wow, they were starting to get antsy from internet withdrawal. Since our team has done a good job of letting customers know they will now need their library card to get on a computer, most have their cards ready. However, "What is my PIN?" is a most frequently asked question during the first few hours. Guest passes are handed out in large quantities for those who missed the announcements about needing a library card. Once logged on, customers have no trouble using the computers.

Customers are able to send print jobs to the printer without any trouble. The questions in this area are about retrieving their printouts and using the print release station, which the library had thought might be a source of confusion. Therefore, an extra staff member is on hand to help at each print release station, and this foresight helps alleviate much frustration at the printer.

Observing the public computers around the library, our project manager is pleased. The system is working as it should. For the most part, the staff members are able to answer questions and assist customers, and customers are accepting the new system. Some are unhappy about having to use a guest pass if they do not have a library card. Others complain that the print release station is too complicated. Only a few comment that they consider the system unnecessary and inconvenient.

The staff at ICPL is doing a remarkable job managing the new system and customer questions. But it certainly helps that the system is working as the staff had been told it would during training. Some staff members are more comfortable with the new system than others, but most are able to assist customers when questions arise.

The initial feedback is positive, and the system is running without any major issues. Our project team deserves congratulations on a successful "go live"! We will get more of their perspective on the launch in the next chapter.

## Endnotes

1.  Bill Keane, *Family Circus* comic strip, August 31, 1994.

# Chapter 11

# Smooth Out the Rough Edges

The system is live, and overall it is working as expected. Some people (both customers and staff, depending on the system) are adapting easily to using the new system, while others need some extra helping hands to get through it. Continue to observe users of the system and listen to their feedback.

## Frequently Asked Questions

Many of the initial questions and concerns about the new system will be procedural in nature. Staff will have to work a little harder to keep track of the steps involved in using the system. Customers using it for the first few times may need reminders on what to do.

Prior to launch, you may have created "how-to" documents to help the staff and/or customers learn the new system. If not, it would be a good idea to do so at this point, at least to assist with the frequently asked questions.

In Chapter 8, I shared the story of the implementation of a cash management system that was derailed due to major holes in functionality. However, the library did manage to complete that installation about a year later and started using the system. When the library finally went live with the system, the circulation supervisors created step-by-step guides for the circulation staff on exactly what steps to follow in order to handle transactions in the new system. The guides were small—one step on each page. They were kept at the circulation desk computers where the new system was installed.

Kudos to them for creating these help guides and providing their staff with a tool to get through the system in the beginning.

It is sometimes easier to get your staff to use help guides than it is to get customers to use them. Often library customers look right past any written directions and turn instead to staff for help. Nonetheless, some basic information can be made available on signs or screens for your public customers. In addition, it can be very helpful to create documentation for your staff to use when they assist customers with the new system. Be sure to provide staff members with some written documentation that they can refer to when faced with questions on the system; it will bolster their confidence with the new system as well.

## Slight Adjustments

As you listen to the feedback and observe use of the new system, now is the time to identify any consistent problem areas. Is there anything that you can do in the configuration of the system or with a supporting tool that might make the system easier to use? Perhaps you can make some spatial changes in the staff or public computer area to help with the workflow. Perhaps you can make some changes on the computer itself, so that it will automatically start up or log in to certain applications.

Here are a few examples:

- After installing new computer and print management software, a library removed a couple of the coin machines for its copiers, intending to have customers use the new system instead. However, the stuff discovered there was a bottleneck at the new coin machine, which was also in use as a print release station as well as a station for customers to put money on their print accounts. The library decided to bring back a couple of its older coin machines for use with the copiers to help alleviate this bottleneck and better accommodate customers.

- After a library migrated to a new ILS, some staff were having trouble viewing the screens, as the font size was less flexible in the new ILS client software. The IT staff provided them with the ability to change their overall screen resolution as needed, which resulted in a larger font for their entire computer. It wasn't a perfect solution, but it did satisfy most staff members.

- A library installed new self-check computers and wanted the bulk of its checkout transactions to go through the new machines. Many tweaks were needed to get the system to provide both flexibility for the customers and security for the library: The length of time that various screens would display before timing out was extended to accommodate the checkout needs of customers; the sound was muted due to confusion about which self-check was "speaking" to which customer; and instructional signage was added to the machines to address some of the patrons' most common mistakes (such as "place item against the back wall"). A self-checkout system is designed for customer use, and each customer is unique. Observing how your library's customers experience the system after going live enables you to customize the settings to best meet your community's needs.

A word of caution, however: You do not want to go into the system and make a lot of sizable changes at this point. Focus on the smaller tweaks to improve the day-to-day processes. Allow ample time (at least three or four weeks) for the staff and/or public users to acclimate to the new system before making many larger changes. As noted throughout this book, adjusting to a new system takes time. Generally speaking, after four to six weeks, the system will have settled in and any major problems that remain could be addressed at that time. Your list of major problems will likely have diminished over that time as well, once the system is given a chance to work.

## Appreciation Goes a Long Way

Some people feel that adjusting to a new system is just part of working in libraries in the 21st century. To some extent, they are right. Libraries are always changing, and library staff members need to be flexible in order to stay current in the industry. Nonetheless, everyone likes to be appreciated—at work, at home, or at play. Therefore, when you have implemented a new system in your library, it never hurts to show your appreciation to your staff for their extra efforts and/or to your customers for their extra patience. Something as simple as a "thank you" provides your staff members or customers with the acknowledgment that a little extra something was required of them at this time and tells them you are grateful. For large new systems, perhaps something beyond a verbal recognition helps sustain the momentum needed to get through the launch. Providing some chocolate, ordering some pizza for lunch, or allowing your staff to dress casually for a day, in addition to sincerely saying "thank you," may ease the way through the transition period.

## Checking In With
## Info City Public Library

Overall, our project team is pleased with how the new system is running. The launch was fairly smooth, as team members had worked hard to plan appropriately and provide information ahead of time to their staff and customers. The implementation specialist from EnvisionWare has left the library, as his job on-site was complete. So it is now up to the staff in the library to support the system locally. Of course, the project manager is still in touch with both the implementation specialist and the support team for assistance whenever needed.

One issue seems to be coming up again and again: A user logs onto the computer with a guest pass and sends a print job, and then cannot remember the auto-generated PIN needed to retrieve the job. The project leader reminds staff how to log in to the print release station as a staff member to assist customers with retrieving their print jobs. Alternatively, if the customer is still logged on to the computer, a staff member can look up the necessary PIN number through the staff interface. Both of these processes are documented and shared as the beginning of a Frequently Asked Questions list on the staff intranet. Many other questions and answers will help this resource grow and provide staff with quick access to answers when needed.

Staff also identify a couple of changes that can be made through the EnvisionWare software to improve their customers' experience:

- Staff have noticed that many customers are not familiar with where the library's various computer areas are located and/or what they are called. So when customers make a reservation for a computer, they often have to ask where that computer is located. EnvisionWare allows for a link to a library map, so staff can decide to create a map of ICPL's computer areas, link to it at the Reservation Stations, and post copies of the map in key areas around the library.

- Customers have increasingly expressed concerns about their privacy. Staff are fielding more and more inquiries as to whether the computer saves customers' logins and passwords. Fortunately, the public computers at ICPL are already configured with software called Deep Freeze; this software keeps the computers in a "frozen" state while the customer is using it, but as soon as the computer is rebooted, *any* changes made are lost. Therefore, any passwords, logins, or downloaded files simply disappear.

Due to the increased security concerns, the IT staff sets
EnvisionWare to reboot at the end of every user session,
and therefore, no customer's privacy will be at risk.

After the first two weeks of using EnvisionWare at ICPL, many of
the staff and customers have settled back into the "business as
usual" routine. Either the majority of the concerns have been
addressed, or the extra chocolate in the staff lounge is keeping
stress levels down.

# Chapter 12

# Take a Look Back

Evaluation is a critical element of any project. Now I'm going to guess that some readers may be rolling their eyes at this point. How many of you have glossed over the evaluation portion of previous projects? Or when required to include it on project plans or grant applications, you simply made it up for the purpose of having *something* written in that section? Truth be told, I have too. I am often faced with getting through one project, only to be pushed on to the next project, without taking a moment to look back. I will address this phenomenon further in the next chapter. But bear with me for now, if you will.

About four weeks after a new system is up and running, many of the kinks are worked out, and the system is stable. Now is the time to look back and review the project. Gather the project team for a final post-implementation meeting. Ask yourselves the hard questions and be honest with the answers.

## The Goal of Evaluation

Are you wondering why this is important, given that we all know many people never do it? The goal here is simply to learn from each project you do and to avoid repeating your mistakes in future projects. Have you ever thought to yourself, "I should have known better!" after repeating a mistake you made on a previous project? I have. It is not necessarily that we did not learn the lesson the first time—we simply get so caught up in each project that we fall back into our usual habits. However, if you were to identify the lessons learned at the end of each project *and review them before starting each new project,* you would be less likely to make the same mistakes again.

# The Hard Questions

There are really only three central questions to ask your team at that final post-implementation meeting, and they are only useful if you answer them honestly:

1. *What worked?* Start by identifying the successes of the project. Where did your team excel? What strengths did your team members bring to the project to help it succeed? Share the achievements across the team and celebrate the accomplishments together.

2. *What did not work?* Next, identify those areas where the project faltered a bit. Did your team fall short in some areas? Were there details missed that should not have been? Did communication break down? Do not place blame on the specific team members involved; the team as a whole contributed to the project's shortcomings.

3. *What could you do better next time?* Finally, list your lessons learned. Note that these should be based on the answers to the first two questions. Lessons are learned from both where the team excelled and where the team faltered. Answers to the first question provide you with the lessons that you will definitely want to consider applying again in future projects. Answers to the second question provide you with the lessons learned after something did not go as smoothly as you had hoped, and these are areas you will strive to improve on for your next project. Ideally, try to come up with six lessons learned— three items from each question.

As you work through these questions as a team, be patient with each other and keep an open mind. Encourage each team member to contribute. Allow time for detailed discussion of the project, but keep the discussion constructive. The goal is to learn honestly from the project so that the next one will go even better.

# Feedback From Others

In addition to your project team's evaluation of the project, you also need to note any feedback you might hear from others more removed from the implementation itself and more involved in using the final product. What are other library staff members saying? What are library customers saying? Be sure to take their feedback to heart.

As we mentioned in Chapter 11, many of the initial trouble spots smooth themselves out in the first few weeks. So by this point, any that remain should be discussed and addressed in the coming weeks or months. Identify the outstanding issues, and identify who on the team will be responsible for following up on these items. If an issue cannot be addressed, identify clearly why not. If a desired functionality is not possible with the system, then at least submit it to the vendor as a suggested enhancement for a future version.

Finally, be sure to identify a process for collecting future feedback about the system. Perhaps your library provides comment cards to your customers. Perhaps you have an intranet or email address where staff suggestions or problem reports are collected. Make sure this resource is made available for your new system as well. Each new system installed at a library provides an opportunity for something to fail. Your library should have a process in place for managing the inevitable moments when something breaks down, and this new system should benefit from the same process in the future.

# Share Your Experience

Share your final evaluation and lessons learned with your library director or the person of authority who initiated the project. Set up a meeting and review how the project went. Highlight the challenges and the successes, and emphasize the important lessons learned. This meeting serves two purposes: It provides a report of the overall project execution, and it allows your director (or other authority figure) a chance to hear the important details of what it took for you and your project team to implement the solution and meet the library's need. During the course of the implementation, there is often no time devoted to communicating to the person in authority about how the project is going. This final meeting brings the project full circle, and with this closure you can move on to your next project.

# Checking In With Info City Public Library

Our project team at ICPL meets once again about four weeks after the system has been implemented for its project review and evaluation meeting. For the most part, the team is satisfied with the system and how it is working at the library. There are no pressing issues, no unresolved problems, and no ongoing sources of stress related to the system. The project is deemed to be a success!

Nevertheless, team members still take time to talk about the hard questions. Without sharing all of the details here, they do identify the following lessons from their project implementation:

1. Their extra efforts during the planning phases of the project truly did pay off in providing them with a solution that met their library's needs. Overall, team members feel they now have a good handle on managing their public computers and providing fair access to their customers.

2. Even though ICPL shared information with its
   community early in the planning process, alerting the
   group to the upcoming downtime of the computers
   and the installation of the new system, the staff
   members recognize that they can never do enough
   promotion and preparation for a system like this. They
   still had many surprised and confused customers, and
   they found themselves answering many of the same
   questions over and over during the first few weeks of
   the system. However, they are pleased that their public
   service staff has been comfortable answering the
   questions and supporting the customers. That staff
   training was very worthwhile.

3. Even though implementation of the basic system went
   smoothly, the team noted that the integration with
   additional equipment and software has been quite
   challenging: setting up copy machines, connecting with
   the library's ILS, and adding peripheral devices (bar code
   scanners, receipt printers, etc.). They had planned for
   some of these things but had not planned fully enough
   for all of them. Some of these associations were not
   covered explicitly in the planning process, and some of
   the details were not even available prior to the
   implementation. The team would like to remember these
   difficulties next time in hopes of smoothing over similar
   rough edges more easily.

The computers at ICPL are in good hands. In the future, the staff
will undoubtedly run into new questions and discover a need for
additional features. But there is a system in place to handle the
current scenarios, and it will set the foundation for future adjustments. On to the next project!

# Are You Ready?

Don't stop reading here—there is one more chapter, and I don't want you to miss out on that. However, if you work in a library where you have more than enough time to implement IT projects and you would never have to cut any corners on the process spelled out in the first 12 chapters of this book, then I suppose you don't need the reality check that follows. (But please contact me. I want to know who you are so I can find out how your library is able to provide you with sufficient time to do everything so completely!)

Chapter 13

# Reality Check

If you are interested in reading this final chapter, chances are you are often pressed for time and want to find out how to be as efficient as possible with your library's technology projects without sacrificing quality. I understand that. Even while writing this book and thinking back over all of the experiences and examples that I discussed here, I often found myself thinking, "Now why can't I just do these things on every project?" Well, the sad reality is that it is just not always possible or even necessary.

Why? Following these steps requires a great deal of time, discipline, and cooperation. And nowadays, how many of us have this kind of time and resources to devote to each project? None, I would guess. We are all doing more with less. And it is not going to get better any time soon. So is all of this really necessary?

Well, the short answer is yes. If you want to be successful, many of the tips outlined in this book are critical to your success. However, not every single step is necessary for every single project. Analyze each project during the planning stages and determine what path makes the most sense to lead you to a successful implementation.

## Must-Haves

No matter what the project is, the following five steps are essential:

1. *Planning:* I must reiterate those wise words, "He who fails to plan, plans to fail." This is not a new concept. Those words have been attributed to many people over the years, and the fundamental truth has not changed. If you

want to achieve something, you have to know where you are going and how you are going to get there. Make a plan. At the very least, create a detailed plan for each project. Go one better: Create a longer term technology plan.

2. *Documentation:* How often do you leave documentation for the last step, and then before you know it, you no longer have time for it because you are on to the next project? Yes, me too. But where does that get you? Lost. Probably not right away, because during and immediately after the project, all the information is still fresh in your mind. After being immersed in any implementation, you likely have all the details right on the top of your head. But how long does it all stay there? A few days, a week or two, if you are lucky ... and then that project's details get replaced by the next task (or problem or email or phone call) and soon you start to wonder how you ever completed that implementation in the first place!

3. *Testing:* Have you ever deployed a new system without testing it or without testing it thoroughly? It's likely you do some testing with each project. To save yourself further headaches, take the time to test as completely as you can. If you do not, your users are guaranteed to find the problems when you let them use the new system. When a user finds a problem, the pressure is that much greater to get it fixed quickly because others are depending on you. Besides, have you ever been that user who found the bugs? If so, you know how frustrating it can be to try to use a system that does not work as it should. Alleviate your users' frustration and your own stress level by taking the time to test before deployment.

4. *Training:* Your project will not be successful if you do not train your staff and your customers (as appropriate) on how to use your new system. In order for any project to be successful, people will have to use the system. If they

cannot use it on their own and find it frustrating as the next "new thing" that is being forced upon them, you may never truly reach a general level of satisfaction. Give your staff the tools needed to understand the new system and to make full use of its capabilities.

5. *Evaluation:* Thought you could leave this one off, too? Well, you can … if you never want to learn from your mistakes or make your future project implementations work more smoothly. After you invest your time and resources into a project, you need to take a look back and see how well those investments paid off for you. Identify what went well, which will give you confidence and motivation for your next project. Identify what could have gone better, which will give you something to strive for on your next project. We all learn something new every day; be sure to give yourself a chance to learn from your own efforts.

# A Mnemonic

When I want to remember something important, I create a mnemonic that provides value in my memory. These five steps are essential to implementing technology solutions in libraries successfully. And they even fit with one of my daily goals: Provide dependable technology to everyone. I believe that phrase sums up my job in many ways, and it also serves as my mnemonic for the five "must have" steps:

Provide: P – Plan
Dependable: D – Document
Technology: T – Test
To: T – Train
Everyone: E – Evaluate

Perhaps that mnemonic will also help you keep the five critical steps in the forefront of your mind when implementing a new IT solution in your library.

# Scale the Steps to Meet Your Project Scope

Each project is unique, just as each library, each community, and each individual is unique. We all have skills to bring to the table, and we all know our own library's needs and our community's dynamic. Therefore, it is up to you to determine how best to implement each project, using the ideas in this book and including the five required steps listed here. Let's look at some sample projects together. This is by no means an exhaustive list of projects, but after looking at these examples, you should be able to adapt the principles defined here for almost any project you implement in your library.

## Redesign Your Website

Many libraries redesign their website every few years. Sometimes the project is a complete overhaul where the entire site is redone with different tools for a different approach. Sometimes the project involves a narrower focus on a few sections of the website. Sometimes the project addresses the aesthetics of the website and simply applies new colors or templates to the website while maintaining the same structure.

Some libraries do the work of a website redesign internally as the staff is responsible for maintaining the website. Alternatively, some libraries hire a third party to handle both the website redesign and the maintenance of the website. Other libraries hire a vendor to do the actual redesign of the website but then have library staff handle the ongoing maintenance internally.

All of these variables will impact the implementation process for the library's website redesign project. However, the five required steps will apply no matter what. And a redesign project will likely include a multiperson project team, so many of the ideas in this book apply directly to this type of project. The planning may be done internally, with a vendor, or both. When a library does a request for proposal (RFP) to find a website design vendor, the project plan must be fully documented as requirements in the RFP. Similarly, if a library is doing the redesign internally, the project team will need to document the requirements and refer back to them throughout the project. Testing is important with a website as well, because broken links or old content pages create a poor user experience.

Training can be done on a variety of levels. You may need to train your staff members on new software that they will use to create and/or maintain the web content. You may need to arrange for training from your vendor to teach your staff how to access the website and modify the content. Even though you will not likely do formal training for your customers on using your new website, you may create an online tutorial to show them how to find information on it. A good website should be designed with an easy-to-use interface, but that does not mean everyone will be able to find everything they need on your new website. So keep these training possibilities in mind before you launch it. In addition, keep the original website around (accessible at least by the staff) in case any content gets missed during the actual migration process.

Finally, evaluation of your new website design is very important. You might want to create online surveys to gather feedback from your online users. You will want to set up some software to collect usage statistics about your website. Take a look at these numbers at least once a month and note what pages your users are visiting often and which ones they might not be visiting at all. This will help you evaluate how useful your website is to your users, so you can make informed decisions about future modifications.

In addition, with a website redesign, there are a few other critical steps. Some projects require definite decisions about how the final project will look. On the other hand, a website needs to have a level of scalability and flexibility built in to the system. By its very nature, a website will need to be updated and possibly even be changed frequently. While you will not likely make major changes, you may want to change what the menus are called, add a menu item, or even add a new menu. Your solution should be flexible enough to allow for minor changes without requiring the entire project to be redone. Even though you will unveil your new website at some point, this project will always be evolving.

Since website designs vary so much and are so flexible, you have a unique opportunity to review many different implementations that others have done and adapt them to your own redesign, and I encourage you to do so. During the research discussions in Chapters 2 and 3, we highlighted some key resources that staff members can use when researching their own solutions. With website design, anything is possible and examples (good and bad) are available in abundance. Often other libraries' websites will provide inspiration, but there also may very well be websites for nonlibrary organizations that offer some unique functionality that you may want to emulate. Website etiquette encourages you to contact the creators of the websites that you admire before imitating their work, but the web is a wonderful collection of possible options.

Finally, even though anything is possible with a website redesign, there are often specific restrictions and/or requirements for a website design project. This is no different from any other project, but due to the creativity that comes to life with this specific type of project, it is all the more important to document the basic requirements in the beginning and keep them handy as the project evolves. It can be frustrating to follow creative ideas down a path, only to discover much later that the path cannot accommodate your requirements.

A website redesign project can be a lot of fun, but people often underestimate the time it requires. Do the planning in the beginning, as with anything else, and you will be able to have fun during the implementation itself.

## Replace Public Computers

A less fun but critically necessary IT project is replacing computers. As much as we would like computers to last a long time, the truth is that they are a disposable resource in libraries, offices, schools, and homes. They do not last forever. In fact, a general rule of thumb for technological stability is to plan to replace/upgrade each computer on a cycle of every three to four years. Certainly budgets often limit this, and IT staff is left trying to keep older hardware functioning for five, six, even seven years. But the technological Band-Aids will only last for a while, and eventually the computers will die and need to be replaced.

Replacing computers is not unique to libraries. However, providing computers for public users is unique. Whether the computers will be used by students in a school or university or by community residents, providing public access computers brings its own collection of computer security challenges. However, many public computers are configured exactly the same way, which makes the management of them a little easier.

Generally, the task of replacing computers falls to the IT staff. However, if new software is being added or the look and feel is being revised, then it is a good idea to include additional public service staff on the project team at some point to get input and provide training.

One element that is distinctive about a computer replacement project is scheduling. In Chapter 5, we talked about scheduling technology projects and ensuring that your users are aware of any time that their access to resources may be interrupted. However, in this "reality check" section, I wanted to address scheduling from a slightly different perspective. How many libraries can actually limit their resources to users while a project is implemented? More often than not, you will not be able to close the library or even make your public computers unavailable for a long period of time.

Therefore, you will have to plan carefully. Your IT staff may need to work outside of normal open hours. You may have to stagger the implementation so as to affect only a few computers at one time. Nonetheless, no matter what parameters constrain the time you have to do the implementation, it is essential that you do not rush over the important steps. Plan so that anyone affected understands the approach and you maintain a high level of quality. You will still need to test and document the project. Rushing to save time at the expense of accuracy will diminish your project's success.

Update your documentation during an upgrade or replacement to keep your IT Inventory current. And you cannot know what you need until you know what you have, so a current IT Inventory is a necessary planning tool. As mentioned in Chapter 5, there is a sample template for an IT Inventory in Appendix E. However, in addition to updating the inventory, you will also want to document the process you take when you set up new computers. Undoubtedly, you will use this process many times. Having it available in writing will make each subsequent pass through the procedure a little easier. And of course, any time you need to update the process, it is important—and very easy—to update the document as well.

Testing is vital when replacing computers. You need to ensure that all the installed software works as it should. You need to have someone try to "break" the computer as well—test the security and determine if there are ways that your public users could get into certain areas of the system and cause harm to the computer, other computers, or your network. In libraries, what public users are allowed to access is often determined by policies. It is important that any new systems are tested to ensure they comply with library policies and provide the library with a stable computing environment. Some libraries are allowed to provide access to many resources, while others have to be more careful. These decisions are made locally and will be different at each library.

Training your public service staff on supporting your new computers is also important. As noted previously, you also might want to include these staff members in the planning process to determine what software is in demand by your public users and to get some ideas for providing the most useful technology resources to meet your library's needs. Some libraries may not support all the actual software installed on their public computers, but at least making staff aware of what is there provides them with a sense of confidence when approached by a user. On the other hand, if you provide classes for your public on how to use the software you install, you will want to make sure that the appropriate staff members are aware of what is new or changed after any upgrades.

Your public users will best be able to provide you with feedback on the new computers, so be sure to provide them with a mechanism to do so. In addition, your public service staff will be most likely to hear customers' feedback and will know the most common questions, so talk to them as well to evaluate your project. You may not be able to provide your public users with everything that they want. Your library's policies will guide your determination of what is possible. But it is always helpful to know what your users want, even if you are unable to meet each and every request.

You may also need to replace staff computers, laptops, servers, or computers that serve other unique purposes. The same principles can apply for just about any hardware replacement or upgrade. You can expand the details to meet the specific situation.

## Accept Credit Card Payments Online

Speaking from experience on this one, I can tell you that this is a project that requires more work than you might initially suspect. Gather a project team that includes people who understand the financial procedures at your library. You will need a financial resource to help translate how the transactions in the software will appear to the bank account and all the steps in between. This particular project challenged me as I had such limited knowledge of how the financial processes worked. It honestly took me about a year to truly understand how all the various pieces had to fit together in order for us to be able to accept online payment of fines and fees. So take ample time to do your homework and talk to others who can help you understand the overall process.

A project like this can generally be implemented with a quiet launch as described in Chapter 10. It is a value-added service, so unless your library board or other governing unit is putting pressure on you to implement it within a certain timeframe, you can likely take the necessary time to understand the process and complete thorough testing before your customers begin using it. And if you find yourself under pressure, do as much homework as you can and communicate with the people in authority about the complexity involved.

Be sure to take the time to shop around on this project. For one thing, you will need a merchant account to process online transactions. Each processor charges a variety of fees, so do your best to find one that has reasonable fees and is willing to work with you. If your software has specific requirements, be sure you understand them. For example, some integrated library system (ILS) vendor software for online payment of fines and fees will only work with specific gateways or merchant processors. Be sure your choices are compatible with your software.

Testing is also particularly important in this type of project. You will need to test the various types of transactions and see how they appear through the various systems. Check with your software vendor and merchant processor, as they should have a test system that you can use to try your transactions so you do not have to use personal credit cards to test your system. And as soon as you start using your system, keep a close eye on your transactions and reports—if you find discrepancies or problems, it is always easier to investigate them sooner rather than later.

Evaluation of a system like this should include more than just the implementation process. It should also include an analysis of the return on investment (ROI). In fact, any new system can be reviewed in light of its ROI. I particularly recommend it with a system that has an impact on your financial processes, such as this one. With online payments, you are paying extra fees to a processing company in the hope that the convenience for your customers will lead to recovery of more fines and fees. If you discover a sub-optimal ROI, that is only one part of the overall picture. However, it is something to monitor, even if your library determines it to be part of the cost of doing business.

Having said all that, I believe that accepting online payments is a very good service, and it is one that more libraries are investigating in the 21st century. It is yet another way that we are challenged to meet our library users where they are, pushing libraries even further beyond where they have been in the past. These challenges constantly push us to grow in the field of information.

## Migrate to a New Integrated Library System

Probably the most massive undertaking for a library is the installation (and migration) of an integrated library system (ILS). The ILS is the lifeblood of the library, and without it, we are lost. We depend on the ILS to know who our customers are and what types of materials we have—and everything else related to either of those items. So, whenever you change it in any way, you risk losing some critical information that everyone depends on.

This is a project where you cannot cut any corners. If you do, your chances of success decrease rapidly. Build a strong project team that includes your key stakeholders. Their input and perspective will help you create a comprehensive plan from the beginning. Plan carefully. Know your library's needs as completely as you can, and investigate any unknowns early on in the process. Talk extensively with prospective vendors about the features and functionality that are most important to your library. Talk with current customers of prospective systems and learn from their experiences. No ILS is perfect, but you have to find one that fits your library. And you have to create a relationship with the vendor that will enable a long-term partnership for providing library service to your community. This is definitely the kind of project where your vendor relationship is extremely important, as highlighted in Chapter 7.

In addition to understanding how important this project is to your library, you need to accept that there will be unexpected hiccups during the implementation. The truth is the larger the project, the more chances there are for something to go wrong. That is why this book includes chapters devoted to taking your pulse mid-project and planning again after you see how things are going. Be prepared to stay flexible. And when things go smoothly because you have planned appropriately, you can be pleasantly surprised and enjoy a little breathing room.

When you are working through an ILS project, it is very important to keep in mind all the additional applications that connect to and depend on your ILS. Do you have self-check machines, computer management software, program registration software, point-of-sale software, online database subscriptions, or anything else that depends on a connection to your patron database? If so, be sure you know how those applications will work after your new ILS implementation. Include all of these dependencies in the beginning of your project planning to ensure they are not forgotten.

Updating documentation diligently through the planning process is especially important in larger projects. There are likely more people involved, and the project will span a longer period of time. During the course of a project, team members will hold pertinent information in their own memories as working knowledge. However, the larger the project and the longer the timeline, the less working knowledge will be available (simply due to the nature of the human brain), so documentation is critical in these projects.

Not surprisingly, careful testing and comprehensive training are absolutely essential. The silver lining, however, is that most vendors of ILSs are well-versed in their systems and especially in testing and training. So you should be able to receive extensive support from your vendor for these steps.

With a project the size of an ILS implementation, take it one step at a time. Choose a vendor that you trust, and trust the process, and you will be successful.

## Add Chat Reference Service

In contrast to some of the larger projects, I wanted my last example to be a fairly small project. Many times IT staff is responsible for implementing projects to support other services at the library. Chat reference is an example of this type of service. Technically, the project is not too complicated. It involves software configuration for the most part. Beyond that, training is the biggest piece.

You will still need to plan appropriately, document the project, and test it. But the majority of the effort in this type of project will be on the training (for staff). And once the system is in use, take the time to evaluate it as always. In this case, it should be fairly easy to get feedback from users about how well it is working (or if it is not).

Smaller projects do have unique challenges, often with regard to the expectations that initiate them. Smaller projects seem like they should not require much time and, therefore, they are often not allotted sufficient time or resources. Anyone who has ever worked with technology will likely agree that any task or project involving technology takes some time to complete, and there are usually at least two attempts before success is achieved. Applying Windows updates, replacing an old cell phone with a new one, creating a report from your ILS, or anything else ... usually there are variables outside your control that impede your progress so you can rarely proceed at the rate you initially intended. That is the nature of technology. So do not fall into the trap of assuming that smaller projects will be straightforward and painless. Sometimes they are but allow enough time to give each project (no matter the size) the time and attention it deserves.

Staff members who work on IT projects in libraries often spend more time on the smaller projects than they do on the larger ones. Sometimes, the work is not even really a project at all—it's troubleshooting a problem, answering a question, or simply helping a user. Those tasks do not require an extensive process. But the values this process emphasizes will be helpful in any task you undertake.

# The Process

As this book outlines a process for implementing technology solutions in libraries, writing it has been a process for me. The ideas outlined here are the ones that have worked for me. You may need to make some adaptations for them to work in your environment. But we are all trying to "Provide Dependable Technology to Everyone" in this information world. You are empowered to do just that. Each day is a new day. So take it one step at a time, and you will find success.

# Sample Technology Plan

**Rochester Hills Public Library Technology Plan 2011–2014**
Prepared by:
Karen Knox, Information Technology Manager
January 2011

## Contents

- Library Mission
- Technology Goals
  - Goals for Public Service
  - Goals for Collection Development
  - Goals for Community Relations
  - Goals for Staff Development and Training
  - Goals for Facilities and Equipment
- Current Status and Equipment Inventory
- Staffing and Training
- Budget Requirements and Projections
- Evaluation

## Library Mission

The goal of this plan is to detail how technology can help the Library fulfill its stated mission: "The Rochester Hills Public

Library provides resources to inform, educate, enlighten and entertain the people of our community."

Increasingly, new technology offers the resources to meet the varied needs of our community. As technology continues to play a vital role in providing access to information, our library users' expectations continue to demand increased access to technology. An integral part of fulfilling our mission is providing materials and resources in electronic formats. Successful integration of technology into our library environment requires ongoing training for all staff. We provide our users with access to information, regardless of the means or the format.

Our technology infrastructure has grown over the years, and it is now quite stable and robust and serves our library needs well. Looking forward, we are faced with decreased revenues, likely for at least five years to come. Therefore, as we must do more with less, we must plan carefully to maintain a balanced and quality of service.

To that end, Rochester Hills Public Library (RHPL) must work to prioritize services and the technology that supports them. The residents in our service area will be our priority, and when we need to scale back due to budget concerns, we will need to shape our technology resources to serve our residents first. It will not be easy to maintain our technology with limited resources. In particular, we want to continue to investigate new technologies and provide high-quality services that our customers expect in the 21st century. This plan is created to maintain what we have and expand to new services, if the funding allows.

# Technology Goals

## Goals for Public Service

Objective 1: Continue to improve methods for accessing information about the Library's materials and customer accounts online through Polaris.

- Add new foreign languages to our self-check machines by December 2011.

- Provide access to a mobile PAC (online catalog) when released in Polaris version 4 by April 2012.

- Investigate notification via text messaging when released in Polaris version 4 by April 2012.

- Maintain access to ChiliFresh, allowing customers to read and write reviews of titles in the Polaris catalog. Explore the new social networking options under development by ChiliFresh to determine if they would provide value to our customers by September 2013.

- Continue to customize interface for Polaris web catalog (ongoing).

- Continue to clean up materials database for Polaris (ongoing).

Objective 2: Continue to improve methods for accessing electronic resources.

- Add Catalog stations to locations closer to the stacks for easy access when searching for print materials by August 2011.

- Explore services available to cell phone users, such as Guide by Cell, by July 2013.

- Create a mobile version of the library's website to optimize usage on a mobile device by December 2013.

- Follow developments by vendors for apps, widgets, and other tools that make access to electronic resources easier, on mobile devices or the web as a whole (ongoing).

- With help from Adult Services, review current collection of electronic databases and evaluate their use, both in the library and remotely (ongoing).

Objective 3: Continue to provide methods for accessing materials that RHPL does not own whenever possible.

- Evaluate usage and costs for OCLC services to ensure appropriate return on investment by December 2011.

- With help from Polaris staff, evaluate the functionality of NCIP for Polaris and MeLCat libraries to improve workflow for MeLCat participation by December 2012.

- Continue participation in MeLCat as funding permits (ongoing).

Objective 4: Maintain and upgrade computer equipment to provide consistent and efficient access to electronic products and services.

- With grant funds, purchase and provide in-building circulation of wireless laptops by September 2012.

- Maintain EnvisionWare software to manage public computers and printing (ongoing).

- Replace/upgrade all public computers to improve performance as funding allows, which may fall outside our previous schedule of every three to four years.

Objective 5: Improve access to library services for customers who do not visit the Main Library on a regular basis.

- Improve internet access from the Bookmobile with Verizon network options by August 2011.

- Support Outreach & Bookmobile Services with the Books by Mail project, and investigate expanding the project through Polaris version 4 by December 2012.

- Explore options for automating circulation at the mini-branches and take advantage of the features available in Polaris by July 2013.

Objective 6: Provide effective training for the public to increase skills with and awareness of electronic products and services.

- Use wireless laptops as a mobile training lab for hands-on internet classes to be offered at the Library or at off-site locations by October 2012.

- Expand availability of recorded video training for customers on website by December 2012.

- With help from Adult Services, continue to offer internet training sessions to the public (ongoing).

Objective 7: Continually improve website functionality and user interface.

- With help from the Web Team, maintain and update the RHPL website with new content and technologies (ongoing).

- Continue to evaluate the user interface and make changes as necessary to provide easier and better access to internet resources (ongoing).

Objective 8: Explore options for providing improved circulation and check-out services to the public.

- If funding allows, install an additional self-check for customer use by October 2013.

- Investigate options for implementing RFID to replace our current electromagnetic security system by November 2013.

- Continue to evaluate the use of the self-check machines and market them for increased usage (ongoing).

## Goals for Collection Development

Objective 1: With the help the librarians and Technical Services staff, provide access to information and materials in Polaris that meets our customers' needs.

- Increase the options for importing records for materials from z39.50 databases, Midwest Tape for other material types, and other vendors as determined by library staff by July 2012.

- Explore using the Polaris Acquisitions module to streamline the ordering process and provide a central source for materials on order for the library by November 2013.

- Track developments in delivery of audio-visual materials to libraries, including ebooks (and readers), movies on flash drives, downloadable music and/or movies, and more. As funding allows and the technology fits, add these new options to the library's collection (ongoing).

- Assist as needed with configuring the import and customization of records to our Polaris database when they are received from vendors or other sources (ongoing).

Objective 2: With the help of the Web Team, expand the Library's website consistent with Library collection development policies.

- Expand the offerings on our website to include online tutorials, online story times, and other interactive content by December 2011.

- With the help of Adult Services, expand our electronic local history materials by digitizing more of this unique material (ongoing).

- Continue to add to the links that are available via our website in an effort to direct our patrons to sites of particular value (ongoing).

Objective 3: Collect statistics on usage of the Library's resources.

- Continue to report statistical information to the board on a monthly basis about usage of our materials and technology and resources (ongoing).

- Monitor statistics provided by electronic database vendors to help analyze product use (ongoing).

## Goals for Community Relations

Objective 1: In conjunction with Adult Services and our Community Relations Specialist, increase the promotion of our electronic resources.

- Continue to offer internet training classes on using Polaris, subscription databases, and other timely topics (ongoing).

- Highlight electronic resources both on our website and in Library publications (ongoing).

Objective 2: Use current technology to promote Library events and services and communicate with our community.

- Maintain and improve our electronic tools for conversations with our community through our email forms and live chat options for customers to communicate with library staff from our website (ongoing).

- With help from the Web Team, continue to promote RHPL's presence on the social networking sites of Facebook and Twitter, and expand the library's use of these tools (ongoing).

- Continue to expand and promote our offerings of enewsletters that are available through BookLetters (ongoing).

Objective 3: Establish partnerships with neighboring libraries and organizations to share in technology endeavors.

- Support the website development needs of the Community Organization Resource Exchange (CORE) by hosting its Events Calendar with the Library's Evanced Solutions software and maintaining both the content and hosting for their website (ongoing).

- Attend meetings with Metro Net and TLN libraries and participate in joint technology projects with these libraries (ongoing).

- Remain active in the Polaris Users Group (PUG) in order to benefit as much as possible from the experiences of other Polaris libraries and the Polaris staff (ongoing).

## Goals for Staff Development and Training

Objective 1: Maintain and upgrade computer equipment to provide consistent and efficient access to electronic products and services.

- Replace/upgrade all staff computers to improve performance as funding allows, which may fall outside our previous schedule of every three or four years.

Objective 2:  Implement technology solutions that improve staff efficiency, communication, and productivity.

- Expand the use of Room Reserve (from Evanced Solutions) to assist staff in scheduling all conference rooms in the library, including those used solely by the staff, by January 2012.

- Implement a solution to schedule the use of shared technology in the library, especially laptops and projectors, by July 2012.

- With the help of the Web Team, continue to update the information available on the staff intranet (Rhub) and provide access to as many resources there as possible (ongoing).

- Maintain and support the use of cell phones and smartphones for key staff members to ensure access when needed (ongoing).

Objective 3: Increase staff competencies in using all appropriate computer resources.

- Create documentation for all staff in use of library technology for basic troubleshooting by November 2013.

- Bring in Polaris staff for refresher training by December 2013.

- Investigate options for offering staff training, both done in-house and by outside groups such as MCLS or MLA (ongoing).

- Create "cheat sheets" for staff to refer to for help with new technology and common problems (ongoing).

## Goals for Facilities and Equipment

Objective 1: Maintain and upgrade the Library's network, telephony, and server technology to provide optimal performance and service for staff and public.

- Upgrade the software for the Library's pass-card security system by July 2011.

- Clean up wiring closets and labeling by November 2011.

- Implement a formalized disaster recovery plan by December 2011.

- Continue with remote data backup of the Library's most critical data in addition to the on-site tape backup rotation (ongoing).

- Sustain sufficient network connectivity and bandwidth to provide access as needed for voice and data for the Library, including planning for upgrades of network lines for either voice or data or both, as needed (ongoing).

Objective 2: Improve methods of communication and management of technology resources at the Library.

- Optimize the process for managing which staff members have access to which technology resources, including streamlining the creation and deletion of these resources, through a single database by December 2011.

- Enhance our internal help-desk solution used by staff to report computer problems to include more features as possible by August 2013.

Objective 3: Create and maintain technology department documentation.

- Inventory all systems and document network, servers, clients, and all related equipment (ongoing).

- Document how to use staff and public computers to provide some written instructions for staff in how to use them (ongoing).

# Current Status and Equipment Inventory

## Local Area Network (LAN)

The Rochester Hills Public Library has a fiber link to the internet, currently provided by AT&T. We increased the bandwidth from 10mb to 20mb in December 2009.

Our LAN connections are managed by Cisco equipment: an ASA 5520, a 3250 core switch, and seven switches (1-2900s and 6-2950s) connected between two wiring closets by fiber.

The Library also maintains a cable modem connection provided by Comcast to support our public wireless network.

Our LAN connections to support our wireless network are managed by a D-Link switch and a Bluesocket Wireless Gateway.

## Servers

We develop, maintain, and upgrade our network. We support the network equipment listed in the previous section with servers.

We installed the infrastructure for a virtual server environment in January 2011. This includes two high-end HP servers running ESX VMWare and one EMC SAN (storage area network) AX4.

In addition to the two ESX servers, we will maintain eight physical servers as needed for key network roles including two domain controllers, four Polaris servers, our mail server, and tape backup server. These other physical servers are running Windows 2003 or 2008. We have migrated t10 of our physical servers to virtual servers on this new infrastructure in order to improve performance, reliability, and management. The virtual servers are running Windows 2003 or 2008.

We maintain two Windows domains, one for staff and one for public. In addition, our web servers reside in a DMZ. These networks are segmented through the Cisco ASA. The servers manage the clients on each network.

## Workstations

We have replaced almost all the computers (and repurposed some lower-usage computers) in the building in the past three years. We have 157 computers total.

Public Computers (82 total):

- Adult Catalog computers (8) – purchased in 2006

- Adult Internet computers (12) – purchased in 2008
- Quiet Computer Room computers (20) – purchased in 2007
- Teen computers (8) – purchased in 2007
- Outreach computers (5) – purchased in 2007
- Youth Internet/Catalog computers (18) – purchased in 2008
- Print Release/Reservation computers (5) – purchased in 2006
- Library Card Registration computers (2) – purchased in 2006
- Self-checkout computers (4) – purchased in 2006

Staff Computers (75 total):

- Adult Services staff computers (10) – purchased in 2007
- Outreach Services staff computers (7) – purchased in 2008
- Bookmobile staff computers (2) – purchased in 2008
- Youth Services staff computers (8) – purchased in 2008
- Circulation Services staff computers (13) – purchased in 2007
- Technical Services staff computers (8) – purchased in 2009
- Service Desk computers (12) – purchased in 2009
- Administration staff computers (6) – purchased in 2008
- IT staff computers (2) – purchase dates vary
- Other: Friends, Staff Lounge, Laptops (7) – purchase dates vary

Total: 157 computers

## Software

Operating systems: The Rochester Hills Public Library uses Windows XP for all of our computers.

Applications: We primarily use the following software applications:

- Microsoft Office 2007 Professional
- Polaris Integrated Library System and Innovative Millennium for MeLCat
- Internet Explorer, Mozilla Firefox, and Public Web Browser

The Library uses a number of other software applications for specific projects.

## Printers and Copiers

We have a variety of printers and copiers being used by staff and public users in our Library.

Public Printers and Copiers (7 total):

- Color printers (2)
- Black and white copiers (4)
- Color copier (1)

Staff Printers and Copiers (24 total):

- Black and white network printers (10)
- Black and white parallel/USB printers (8)
- Color printers (1)
- Black and white copiers (5)

## Telephony

We have two PRI lines and DS1 service on those lines, including a block of DID numbers. We also have 2 POTS lines and an analog alarm trunk. AT&T is our telephone service provider for local and long distance. We have an Avaya Merlin Magix traditional telephone system with voice mail. The library has 70 telephone handsets.

# Staffing and Training

## Current Staffing

The technology for the library is managed by the Information Technology Manager, a full-time librarian who manages IT, Technical Services, and Circulation Services.

For IT, the library has two part-time Computer Systems Technicians to assist the IT Manager. These positions provide computer support for the entire library. For larger projects, some help from contract IT staff is necessary.

Technical Services is staffed by a full-time department head, 4 full-time clerks, and 1 part-time clerk. Circulation Services is staffed by a full-time department head, 3 full-time clerks, 6 part-time clerks, and a number of hourly clerks. The Head of Circulation also assists in the system administration of our Polaris database.

## IT Staff Training

The field of technology changes so rapidly that continuing education and training is essential. In order to fulfill the goals outlined in this plan, training in more advanced topics will be necessary.

## Library Staff Training

With the continued introduction of updated hardware and software, library staff members need frequent training updates and refreshers to help keep their skills current. They also need more advanced level training to help them use computers more efficiently and effectively. In particular, our staff members need more training on Windows, our subscription databases, Polaris, and help using much of the software applications. Our Internet Librarian offers learning lunches to help provide learning opportunities for staff. When available, staff is able to attend training classes and conferences outside the library, including the Michigan Library Association conference, workshops at the Michigan Library Association and the Michigan Library Consortium, and national conferences including the Public Library Association conference and the Computers in Libraries conference.

## Consulting and Design Services

The Library frequently employs the services of network consultants to assist with design, planning, and implementation of complex projects such as new server installation or major network upgrades.

# Budget Requirements and Projections

## 2011 (4% Total Budget Decrease Over 2010)

| Project planned | Total cost |
|---|---|
| *IT Equipment* | |
| Servers for Polaris and virtualization | $15,000 |
| Grant match for wireless laptops | $2,000 |
| Computer upgrades/replacements | $23,000 |
| Smaller IT equipment/supplies/maintenance | $25,000 |
| Category subtotal: | $65,000 |
| | |
| *Equipment/Systems Maintenance* | |
| Polaris maintenance | $33,000 |
| Postal meter maintenance | $2,700 |
| Telephone system maintenance | $1,000 |
| Photocopier maintenance | $3,500 |
| Category subtotal: | $40,200 |
| | |
| Voice and Data Network Connectivity: | |
| Phone (including wireless cell) | $25,800 |
| Internet | $31,000 |
| Category subtotal: | $56,800 |
| | |
| *Software Maintenance and Support* | |
| Symantec anti-virus | $5,500 |
| Cisco firewall, switches | $1,700 |
| Spam solution for staff email | $2,700 |

| | |
|---|---|
| Websense filter software | $1,025 |
| Deep freeze rollback software on public computers | $200 |
| Public web browser | $50 |
| EnvisionWare PC/print management software | $5,800 |
| ITG self-check maintenance | $6.900 |
| Peek-a-book | $1,200 |
| Early literacy station | $400 |
| Evanced calendar | $4,000 |
| ChiliFresh renewal | $1,200 |
| OCLC Resource Sharing and CatExpress | $3,500 |
| Category subtotal: | $34,175 |
| | |
| *Staff Training* | |
| Public Library Association conference attendance | $2,000 |
| MLA/MCLS workshops/conference attendance | $2,000 |
| Polaris Users Group conference | $2,000 |
| Category subtotal: | $6,000 |
| | |
| **2011 Technology Budget Total** | **$202,175** |

## 2012 (12% Total Budget Decrease Over 2011)

| Project planned | Total cost |
|---|---|
| *IT Equipment* | |
| Budget for emergency equipment needs | $5,000 |
| Smaller IT equipment/supplies/maintenance | $25,000 |
| Category subtotal: | $30,000 |
| | |
| *Equipment Maintenance* | |
| Polaris maintenance | $34,000 |
| Postal meter maintenance | $2,700 |
| Telephone system maintenance | $1,000 |
| Photocopier maintenance | $3,500 |
| Category subtotal: | $41,200 |
| | |
| *Voice and Data Network Connectivity* | |
| Phone (including wireless cell) | $23,000 |
| Internet | $18,000 |
| Category subtotal: | $41,000 |
| | |
| *Software Maintenance and Support* | |
| Symantec anti-virus | $5,500 |
| Cisco firewall, switches | $1,700 |

| Spam solution for staff email | $1,500 |
|---|---|
| Websense filter software | $1,100 |
| Deep freeze rollback software on public computers | $200 |
| Public web browser | $50 |
| EnvisionWare PC/print management software | $5,800 |
| ITG self-check maintenance | $6,900 |
| Peek-a-book | $1,200 |
| Early literacy station | $400 |
| Evanced calendar | $4,000 |
| ChiliFresh | $1,200 |
| OCLC Resource Sharing and CatExpress | $3,500 |
| MozyPro | $700 |
| Category subtotal: | $33,750 |
| | |
| *Staff Training* | |
| Computers in Libraries conference attendance | $2,000 |
| MLA/MCLS workshops/conference attendance | $2,000 |
| Polaris Users Group conference | $2,000 |
| Category subtotal: | $6,000 |
| | |
| **2012 Technology Budget Total:** | **$151,950** |

# Evaluation

Evaluation is a key part of this Technology Plan:

- The IT Manager will review progress on projects in this plan every three (3) months.

- Each goal and objective in this plan has a deadline, and it is the IT Manager's responsibility to ensure that projects are completed in their scheduled timeframe or adjusted according to library needs and priorities.

- The IT Manager will remain aware of evolving technologies that may benefit RHPL by her participation on email discussion lists, attendance at conferences and workshops, and networking with others through The Library Network, Metro Net, and other consortia (ongoing).

- When a new project presents itself that could benefit RHPL, the IT Manager will work with the Library Director to determine if we can pursue the project and if there is a way to budget for the project within the current or a future fiscal year.

- The IT Manager will meet with other library managers and the Director annually to discuss progress of the Technology Plan.

- The IT Manager is responsible for keeping the plan current throughout the length of the plan and creating a new one every three (3) years.

- The IT Manager will meet with other library managers and the Director annually to discuss progress of the Technology Plan.

- The IT Manager is responsible for keeping the plan current throughout the length of the plan and creating a new one every three (3) years.

# Sample Request for Proposal

## General Conditions

The Rochester Hills Public Library is soliciting bids from qualified vendors for a Closed Circuit Television System for the Library located at 500 Olde Towne Road, Rochester, Michigan 48307.

The following request for proposal (RFP) is being provided to you for your consideration. To be considered, your company must meet the qualifications and satisfy the requirements set forth in this RFP.

* * *

Karen Knox
IT Manager
Rochester Hills Public Library
500 Olde Towne Road
Rochester, Michigan 48307
248-650-7123

Final proposals must be received at the address noted above by 5:00 PM on Wednesday, September 7, 2011. Although cost will be an important factor in awarding the contract, the Library is not obligated by any statute or regulation to award the bid for the Closed Circuit Television Surveillance System on the basis of cost. Accordingly, the Library reserves the right to evaluate all proposals objectively and subjectively and to accept or reject any or all proposals or portion thereof. Additionally, the Library reserves the right to negotiate changes in equipment with the company determined to have submitted the proposal that is in the best interest of the library.

It is to be understood that this RFP constitutes specifications only for the purpose of receiving proposals for services and does not constitute an agreement for those services.

The information contained herein is believed to be accurate, but it is not to be considered in any way as a warranty.

All questions, clarifications, and correspondence should be directed to Karen Knox at the address noted above or by telephone.

# Withdrawal of Proposals

Proposals shall remain valid for a period of thirty (30) days after submission. Modifications to proposals will not be accepted by the Library, except as may be mutually agreed upon following the acceptance of the proposal.

# Timetable

RFP released: August 4, 2011
Mandatory walk-through: August 15, 2011, 10:00 AM
Deadline for receipt of bids: September 7, 2011
Recommendation to Library Board: September 21, 2011
Notification to all vendors as soon as possible after
    September 21, 2011

# Requirements

Bid specifications for the Closed Circuit Television System must match specifications on the bid sheet or be of equal specifications to be accepted. Please include all cost factors and a specific delivery time frame.

# Method of Evaluating Proposals

After the bids have been evaluated, cost and other considerations will be evaluated. Once all factors have been evaluated, the Vendor that is the lowest responsive, responsible bidder will be selected for recommendation to the Library Board.

# Payment

Final Payment to the successful bidder will be paid upon completion of delivery, installation of the product, and successful configuration and implementation of the equipment.

# Notice of Nondiscrimination

The Rochester Hills Public Library does not discriminate on the basis of race, color, national origin, sex, age, religion, height, weight, marital status, or disability in its programs and activities. The following person has been designated to handle inquiries regarding the nondiscrimination policies:

Christine L. Hage, Director
Rochester Hills Public Library
500 Olde Towne Road
Rochester, MI 48307
248-650-7122

# Part 1: General

## Description of Work: Base Bid

Provide labor, material, and equipment to provide and install a closed circuit television (CCTV) video surveillance system to cover entrances, internal areas, and exterior areas at one building for the Client as specified. The system will include a combination of indoor and outdoor fixed-view, high-resolution color cameras. The system will include remote viewing capabilities that will provide for viewing of live and recorded video at client workstations.

## Vendor Will Provide

- All equipment and installation to constitute a fully operational CCTV surveillance system

- DVR at the Main Library

- CCTV cameras

- Any necessary transmitters and receivers

- Power supplies (includes power supplies for exterior cameras/heaters/blowers)

- Cabling and cross connection to provide complete circuit from camera location to DVR head-end at the library

- Software for remote management of CCTV system– preferably web-based remote access

- All horizontal and backbone cabling to connect cameras to equipment room locations, in accordance with final design specifications

- Cable from connection point to vicinity of camera final location

- Cabling to be tested and certified to standards; provide documentation

- Jacks, connectors, ties, clamps, conduit, BNC connectors, plenum cable, and other network supporting hardware as needed to support specified equipment

- Backbone cabling to DVR location

- Final termination at control end of system

- Final aiming, focusing, and adjusting of all cameras

- Programming of DVR to include camera names, user/operator data and permissions, basic recording settings, remote access settings, and other programming as needed to make the system operational

- On-site training for client users, in accordance with client work schedule

- Technical support for a period of at least one (1) year commencing at the completion of training at no additional charge. This will include over-the-phone and site visits as needed

- One (1) year warranty on all parts and equipment (except cabling) at no additional charge

## Client Will Provide

- 110 AC power circuit at the DVR location

## Camera Locations

- Public south entrance facing door

- Public west entrance facing door

- Staff south entrance facing door

- Exterior of drive-up window on south side

- Exterior area of bike racks on west side

- Outside area of entrance to public restrooms on first floor in west entryway

- Circulation workroom sorting and check-in area on first floor

- Cash drawers at circulation desk on first floor

- Youth services computer area on west end of first floor

- Youth services ExploreZone area on first floor

- Outside area of entrance to public restrooms on second floor

- Teen computer area on second floor

- Computer area on east end of second floor

# Part 2: Products

## Materials

- All equipment, components, wire, cable, and mounting hardware are to be provided and installed as required to meet manufacturer's specifications and documented installation procedures.

- All materials and equipment shall be standard, regularly manufactured equipment. All systems and components shall be thoroughly tested and proven in actual field use. Whenever components are included from sources other than the manufacturer, the Vendor shall demonstrate and verify that the components are compatible, prior to system acceptance, and shall provide to the Library that use of such components will not void the system warranty.

- Work shall be performed in accordance with the applicable international, federal, state, and local codes, or standards current at the commencement of installation. Where more than one code or regulation is applicable, the more stringent shall apply.

- Cable installation, identification, and termination shall be performed in accordance with the manufacturer's technical installation guidance, in addition to applicable codes above.

- In the absence of manufacturer recommendations on conductor application, the Vendor shall ensure that the cable selected meets all technical requirements of the equipment to be installed.

## Parts List: Base Bid

| Qty | Description | Price |
|-----|-------------|-------|
| 1 | DVR that meets the following specifications:<br>• 16 channels<br>• 500 GB hard drive<br>• 320 x 240 pixels (CIF) at 120 fps.<br>• Offer a full multi-user authorization logon function<br>• Include a Central Monitoring Software application for remote access<br>• Include a CD-RW or DVD+RW optical drive and USB flash drive for saving clips of recorded data<br>• Include a customer 3-year limited warranty | |
| 11 | Indoor color dome camera that meets the following specifications:<br>• Intensifier built-in (selectable from 2x to 128x) for day/night operation<br>• 1/3 inch color CCD imaging device w/customized DSP<br>• 2.8 to 11mm DC auto iris varifocal lens<br>• Horizontal resolution of 540 TV lines<br>• Minimum illumination of 0.002 Lux (intensifier)/0.03 Lux (shutter)<br>• Power supply of 12V DC & 24A VC (dual voltage)<br>• White housing | |
| 2 | Outdoor color dome camera that meets the following specifications:<br>• Intensifier built-in (selectable from 2x to 256x) for day/night operation<br>• 1/3 inch color CCD imaging device w/customized DSP<br>• 2.8 to 10mm DC auto iris varifocal lens<br>• Horizontal resolution of 580 TV lines<br>• Minimum illumination of 0.002 Lux (intensifier)/0.03 Lux (shutter)<br>• Power supply of 12V DC & 24A VC (dual voltage) | |
| 1 | Power supply for cameras that meets the following specifications:<br>• Rack mount chassis<br>• 24VAC @ 12.5 amp<br>• Thirty-two (32) Class 2 Rated PTC protected power limited outputs | |
| | Wiring and mounting for cameras:<br>• Use RG6 CATV 75 Ohm coaxial cable<br>• For termination, use Leviton QuickPort Compression F-Connectors | |

| | |
|---|---|
| | • For connectors, use true 75 Ohm BNC adapters with gold-plated (15 micro–inches) contacts and PTFE insulation material (not delrin)<br>• For fire stopping, use Smooth Penetrator (SP-1, SP-2, and/or SP-4) from Unique Fire Stop Products | |
| | Installation labor for cameras, connected to cabling | |
| | Installation labor for head-end equipment, per specification; includes mounting equipment, connecting cameras to cabling, programming, training | |
| | Additional installation supplies (cable support, etc) – please specify: | |
| | Additional labor or equipment – please specify: | |
| | Shipping/Freight/Transportation charges | |
| **Installed Total** | | |

# Accepted Manufacturers

*General Note:* All quoted equipment must meet or exceed the specifications listed in this bid on pages 6 and 7. These manufacturers are supplied as a guideline for bidders, based on equipment that the library is familiar with.

DVR:

- Speco
- Sony
- Pelco

Cameras:

- Speco
- Sony

- Pelco

- Nuvico

- Phillips/Burle

- Bosch

Power supplies:

- Altronix

- Bosch

- Pelco

*Substitution Note:* Bidders are responsible for ensuring compliance with specifications and are encouraged to provide a complete apples-to-apples comparison with equipment listed above. Bidders are responsible for detailing any equipment that is not an exact match to parts listed above. Bidders must provide a complete part number for any substituted equipment along with cut sheets and manufacturer's specifications for evaluation by client.

# Part 3: Execution

## Installation

- All equipment are to be installed as specified in accordance with project specifications and manufacturer's recommendations.

- All wire routes will be conducted utilizing concealed spaces to the greatest extent possible. In the event cable or wire cannot be concealed in existing structural areas, wire and cable will be routed at the highest point available. Conduit or similar protected chases will be utilized on all vertical runs to surface-mounted devices.

- Control panels and devices shall be rack-mounted as applicable by manufacturer's recommendation. Surface mount panels, if any, shall be mounted utilizing appropriate bracing and anchoring. All terminal blocks, control panels, wire junction points, etc., will be fully enclosed in manufacturer's recommended enclosures. Exterior-mounted devices shall be mounted in NEMA-rated enclosures as applicable.

- All wire and cable will be appropriately labeled and marked at termination points, clearly identifying the line and its intended use. All mid-point terminal or junction points will be labeled appropriately. Any punch-throughs, or other breaches in fire separation barriers, will be appropriately re-sealed upon completion of the wire runs.

- Prior to termination, Vendor will verify, by industry-recognized standards and manufacturer's recommendations, the reliability of wire runs, testing for opens, shorts, ground-loops, etc.

- Prior to initial start-up of the system, Vendor will ensure all components are appropriately grounded and shielded according to manufacturer's recommendations and industry standards.

- Vendor will conduct initial start-up and will conduct full functional testing of the system and its components. In the event problems are identified and, in the opinion of Library, Vendor is unable to sufficiently address a technical malfunction, the appropriate manufacturer's representative will be contacted and made available if necessary, at no cost to Rochester Hills Public Library.

- Upon completion of initial start-up and testing, Vendor will conduct initial programming of the system as described previously. Vendor will work with Library staff to ensure all appropriate information is input appropriately to make the system operational.

## Programming

- Vendor will be responsible for all initial programming of the system including naming all points in the system, establishing basic recording parameter and time schedules, and any other parameters in order to make the system operational.

- Vendor will assist Rochester Hills Public Library in setting up the system. Vendor will identify required data and will provide forms or other data gathering devices to the Library for the purpose of initial system programming. Library staff will be responsible for gathering the required data and providing it to Vendor in sufficient time to meet schedules.

## Training and Testing

- Vendor will be responsible for providing training to a group of key Library employees on the basic operation and maintenance of the system. The training shall be sufficient to allow Library staff to operate the system independent of outside assistance.

- Vendor will provide all users manuals and other training documents on the specifics of the system to accomplish training and operational requirements.

- Vendor will provide additional technical assistance as needed on the basic operation of the system for the entire term of the warranty at no additional charge to Library.

- Vendor will conduct and document a final performance test of all components to validate system operability.

## Warranty Information

- Camera system components are covered for replacement and/or repair of defective components by manufacturer's warranty subject to specific conditions as directed by manufacturer.

- Vendor will cover all labor related expenses to warranty-covered service calls for the period of at least ninety (90) days commencing at the completion of training at no additional charge.

# Sample Review Tool

**Security Camera Proposals Reviewed**
Vendor:
Date:
Reviewer:

Rate the following criteria on a scale from 1 to 4, where 1 = Strongly Disagree, 2 = Disagree, 3 = Agree, and 4 = Strongly Agree. If the criteria was not addressed in the proposal, use a rating of 0 for those items.

| Criteria | Rating (1 to 4) |
|---|---|
| Materials proposed meet requested specifications | |
|    DVR | |
|    Indoor cameras | |
|    Outdoor cameras | |
|    Power supply | |
|    Wiring and mounting | |
|    Additional materials are specified | |
|    Warranty information is included | |
| Installation | |
|    Workers are professional and qualified for the job | |
|    Vendor will provide tools and supplies that meet the requested specifications | |
|    Installation will be completed in a timely fashion | |
| Configuration | |
|    Vendor will configure all cameras for optimal image capture and quality | |
|    Vendor will configure DVR for optimal recording, storage of content, and secure access to stored video | |
| Vendor will thoroughly test | |
|    Each camera | |
|    The DVR | |
|    The power supply | |

| Vendor will provide training to staff on | |
| --- | --- |
| Configuring the DVR | |
| Accessing stored video content | |
| Exporting stored video content | |
| Providing remote access to the DVR system | |
| Overall proposal | |
| Vendor included a solution for all requested items | |
| Vendor included additional specification sheets, photos, and details for proposed solutions | |
| Vendor has reliable references with other customers | |
| Vendor demonstrates sincere interest in working with RHPL | |

Answer the following questions, using 1 for yes and 0 for no:

| Criteria | Rating (1 or 0) |
| --- | --- |
| Cost | |
| Vendor proposed quality materials, which resulted in a higher cost | |
| Vendor proposed inferior materials, which resulted in a lower cost | |
| Vendor proposed quality materials at a reasonable cost | |
| Vendor met bid requirements | |
| Bid was submitted before deadline | |
| Vendor attended walk-thru | |
| Vendor's response went beyond the basics to provide additional value to RHPL | |

Total Score:

Comments:

Use the total score in a spreadsheet to compare the responses. Note that this is a sample tool, and other criteria may be important when reviewing proposals for each project.

# Sample Recommendation for Vendor Solution

**Security Cameras—CCTV Systems**
Recommendation provided by Karen Knox, IT Manager, RHPL,
September 14, 2010

## Background

- RHPL created a request for proposal (RFP) for a CCTV system. It was listed for a DVR, 13 cameras (11 indoor and 2 outdoor), a power supply, all required cabling and adapters that meet required specifications, installation, configuration, training, and one-year maintenance.

- This RFP was sent directly to seven vendors, posted to a couple of library email lists, and posted on our website.

- We had a mandatory walk-through at RHPL that was attended by 10 vendors.

- We received nine bid responses.

## Recommendation

After much analysis, I have determined that the preferred vendor for this project is Aegis Concepts, for the following reasons:

- RHPL has worked with Aegis Concepts in the past for cabling projects and phone system management. We have always had a very positive experience with the company.

- Aegis Concepts submitted a very complete bid, itemizing each item carefully so we know exactly what the costs will be.

- Aegis Concepts bid all requested equipment, preferred manufacturers, and quality materials that meet required specifications.

- Aegis Concepts included qualifications and certifications of staff members who would be handling the installation.

- In terms of cost, Aegis Concepts fell in the middle of the range of bids (from $7,295 to $17,995). However, I eliminated many of the bids at the lower end of the range due to the following shortfalls:

  - Some of the submitted bids did not meet the required specifications.

  - Some of the submitted bids did not include the preferred equipment manufacturers.

  - Some of the submitted bids did not include everything that was requested.

  - Some of the submitted bids were not itemized at all, so it's nearly impossible to tell what we would be paying for.

Therefore, after careful consideration and analysis of quality of materials, cost of entire project, trust in the vendor, and ensuring that the end product will meet RHPL's needs, I recommend that we award the project to Aegis Concepts for a total bid cost of $15,717.

# IT Inventory Template

I keep my IT Inventory in an Excel workbook with individual work-sheets for the following major categories, with the subheadings under each on the sheet itself:

- Staff computers
    - Computer name
    - Primary user login
    - Location (department)
    - IP address
    - MAC address
    - Make
    - Model
    - Serial number/product number/service tag
    - Size of hard drive
    - Amount of RAM
    - Processor speed
    - Optical drive
    - Date of purchase
    - Warranty begin/end
    - Network drop number
    - Peripherals attached
    - Notes

- Public computers
  - Computer name
  - Primary user login
  - Location (department)
  - IP address
  - MAC address
  - Make
  - Model
  - Serial number/product number/service tag
  - Size of hard drive
  - Amount of RAM
  - Processor speed
  - Optical drive
  - Date of purchase
  - Warranty begin/end
  - Network drop number
  - Peripherals attached
  - Notes
- Printers
  - Share name
  - Location (department)
  - IP address
  - Make
  - Model
  - Driver

- Date of purchase
- Warranty begin/end
- Network drop number
- Notes

- Servers
  - Server name
  - Location
  - IP address
  - MAC address
  - Make
  - Model
  - Serial number/product number/service tag
  - Size of hard drive
  - Amount of RAM
  - Processor speed
  - Optical drive
  - Date of purchase
  - Warranty begin/end
  - Network drop number
  - Notes

- Network equipment
  - Device name
  - Location (department)
  - IP address
  - MAC address

- Make

- Model

- Serial number/product number/service tag

- Date of purchase

- Warranty begin/end

- Network drop number

- Notes

• Software

- Name of software

- Version of software

- Number of licenses

- License key

- Maintenance expiration date

- Location(s) where installed

• Vendor contact information

- Company name

- Contact name

- Product(s) supported

- Phone number(s)

- Email address

- Mailing address

- Fax number

- Notes

In addition, you might want to include a worksheet for the following:

- Equipment in storage: either prepare for deployment or out of service

- Telephones: include wireless as well

- Other specialty equipment (vending devices, scanners)

Passwords must also be documented but as securely as possible. Use a tool that will help you store and manage your passwords. I use a free product called 4UOnly from Dillobits software, available online at www.dillobits.com/4uonly.html. This tool allows you to store usernames and passwords for any purpose, and it includes features for writing notes, auto-generating passwords, and setting passwords to expire on a certain date. It requires one password to open the master password file, so you must remember that one, but the rest are safely stored for you.

# IP Planner Template

| Example Customer: IP Address Assignments | | | | | | | |
|---|---|---|---|---|---|---|---|
| Address<br><br>Range/Subnet/Node | | | Description | | | | |
| 38.54.212.48 /30 | | | Access circuit from UUNet to access router | | | | Use the slash /# notation to designate a mask value for the network |
| | | .49 | | | | UUNet distribution router | |
| | | .50 | | | | Access router (cisco 2611) cust-rtr | |
| 196.125.14.0 [24] | | | Public address block assigned by UUNet (ISP) | | | | |
| | 196.125.14.0 /24 | | Internet access, Ethernet segment outside the firewall | | | | |
| | | .0 .0- .15.0 | | | External (to the firewall) nodes | | |
| | | .1 | | | ISP access router | | |
| | | .2 | | | PIX firewall (outside) interface | | |
| | | .4 | | | Innocent victim server (kill-me-srvr) | | |
| | | .128 -<br><br>.254 | | | Global NAT pool | | |
| 10.0.0.0 [8] | | | Private addr block for all internal networks | | | | Use the box [#] notation to designate a reservation of IP addresses (designating the value by # of bits in the address prefix). |
| 10.1.0.0 [16] | | | Site 1, reserved for new HQ location | | | | |
| 10.2.0.0 [16] | | | Site 2, current HQ, future mfg operations center | | | | |

| 10.2.1.0/24 | | | Internal Network (1st floor, switched Ethernet) |
|---|---|---|---|
| | .1.0-.10.0 | | Reserved for servers |
| | | .1 | hq1-site, site router (Cisco 4500M) |
| | | .2 | SBend, NT server |
| | | .3 | SBendNW, NetWare 5 server |
| | | .10 | TRAIN, training server, NetWare 4.11 server |
| | .21.0-.254.0 | | |
| | | .21 | DHCP assigned, addr to SB-Laser |
| | | .20-.254 | DHCP scope on NT-SB server |
| | | | |
| 10.2.4.0/26 | | | Internal Network (2nd floor, switched Ethernet) |
| | 10.2.4.0 [24] | | Reserved for printers |
| | | .1 | Printer 1, SW corner, color laser |
| | | .2 | Printer 2, SW corner, HS laser |
| | | | |
| | .5.0 - .7.0 | | Reserved for workstations |
| | | .5.1 - .7.254 | DHCP pool (ucrp-north) |
| | | excl .5.18 | exclude workstation address (hard addressed for host) |

> Use the slash /# notation to designate a mask value. This would normally be designated in the second column (make sure you use 0's in the node bit positions).

> Ranges for various devices can be designated by prefix (preferred when on a binary boundary) or by designating the range.

> Only individual node addresses (.34), node ranges (.1 - .254) or exclusions (excl .5.18) should be located in the rightmost address column.

# Column Position and Various Recommendations

- Address assignments from outside agencies (parent company, ISP) or global design (selection of private address space).

- Address reservations for sites, locations, and major facilities.

- Designate address mask value.

- Designate reservation within a network (most likely based on the functional role of the IP node).

- Formally assign IP addresses to nodes (could be individual addresses or a range such as a DHCP pool).

- The first two columns are formatted **bold** for easy recognition of major address reservations and reference to the address mask value.

- The far right column (description) is formatted with wrap turned on for verbose descriptions.

# What Attributes Are Associated With a Good IP Address Plan?

- Well-documented, in the form of a living document

- Hierarchical

- Scalable

- Facilitates native IP properties and behaviors (binary boundaries)

# What Information Is Documented in the IP Address Plan?

- Formal address assignments either as a part of the design decision process (your choice of 10.0.0.0) or by assignment from an outside organization such as an ISP or a parent organization

- Address reservations for significant items such as locations, classes of equipment or security zones

- Mask values to be assigned during node implementations

# About the Author

**Karen C. Knox** is the IT manager at the Rochester Hills Public Library (RHPL) in Rochester, Michigan. She has found her niche in library technology—it was the perfect combination of her computer science skills and her love for libraries. She has a BS in computer science from the University of Michigan and an MLIS from the University of Texas at Austin. She has worked with technology in public libraries in Michigan for about 10 years, including five years before RHPL at the Novi Public Library in Novi, Michigan. Her first job upon being hired at RHPL was to lead the migration project from its previous ILS to Polaris. Nothing like hitting the ground running! But truth be told, she embraces the challenges … not necessarily the stress, but the challenges.

Karen enjoys being involved in the library profession and has held various positions in the Michigan Library Association. She currently chairs the Polaris Users Group. She has presented at conferences and published articles on a variety of library technology topics. She thoroughly enjoys how "library people" are so willing to share ideas with one another.

In her spare time, Karen enjoys reading chick lit, solving Sudoku puzzles, watching *Law & Order*, and playing PopCap games. She is addicted to her CrackBerry at times but finds relief with the tunes on her MP3 player. She always enjoys writing, as it provides her with an outlet for her thoughts. She also loves children's literature, and once considered becoming a children's librarian. Karen can often be found spending time with her wonderful family and friends and looks forward to many more adventures in her life!

# Index